GARLAND STUDIES ON

THE ELDERLY IN AMERICA

edited by

STUART BRUCHEY
UNIVERSITY OF MAINE

A GARLAND SERIES

THE POLITICS OF PHYSICIAN ASSISTED SUICIDE

NINA CLARK

GARLAND PUBLISHING, Inc.
NEW YORK & LONDON / 1997

ABF 3202

Library of Congress Cataloging-in-Publication Data

Clark, Nina, 1966–
    The politics of physician assisted suicide / Nina Clark.
        p.   cm. — (Garland studies on the elderly in America)
    Includes bibliographical references and index.
    ISBN 0-8153-2645-9 (alk. paper)
        1. Assisted suicide—Government policy—United States.
2. Assisted suicide—Law and legislation—United States.
3. Assisted suicide—United States—Public opinion   I. Title.
II. Series.
R726.C553 1997
179.7—dc21   96-48392

Printed on acid-free, 250-year-life paper
Manufactured in the United States of America

For my mom, Roma

Contents

Figures and Tables

Foreword

The winds of change are blowing across the deathbeds of America. By the turn of the century, after twenty-five years of hot debate—sometimes compassionate and intelligent, often dogmatic and bitter—we shall be in a new era of death by choice for those who would rather not suffer unbearably when they are assuredly dying.

The circumstances and events which have brought about this seminal change from two thousand years of Judeo-Christian tradition that suicide of any kind was a mortal sin were mainly the following:

- The introduction of high-technology medicine (including sophisticated drugs) which often defeated the specter of death but reduced quality of life.

- A better educated and informed public now capable (through the expanded news media not available to our grandparents) of making up its own mind on issues of medical decisions and ethics.

- The rise from 1980 onwards of a militant right-to-die movement campaigning consistently, and with high visibility, for change in attitudes and laws relating to justifiable assisted death.

- The publicity-driven, maverick campaign commencing in 1990 of Dr. Jack Kevorkian to destroy the official myth that doctors must never kill no matter how much their patients are suffering.

- The publication and rise to the bestseller lists in 1991 of *Final Exit*, making easily available to the public a manual by which terminally ill patients could—with or without a doctor's aid—take their own lives if they wished.

- Voters' ballot initiatives in three West Coast states asking for lawful physician-assisted dying, the last of which (Oregon, 1994) was successful.

- Landmark rulings by both the 9th and 2nd Circuit Courts of Appeal (1996) which agreed that existing states' laws prohibiting physician-assisted suicide were unconstitutional. Whether or not these rulings are eventually overturned, the impact of arguments cogently made by some twenty-seven high court judges remain historic.

In the 1980s the arguments concerning hastened death revolved around whether or not the procedure was ethical. In the next decade, with public opinion moving as high as 70 percent in favor, the arguments switched to whether or not it could be successfully regulated by law or better left to the medical profession to self-regulate.

Yet anther debate broke out over whether the courts could or should not only approve acceptance but also sanction the criteria for physician-assisted suicide. Could a small group of non-elected jurists fix a nation's social and ethical policy? Sometimes in the American democratic system, the issues are so divisive—abortion and gay rights are the best modern examples—that the high courts have no choice but to step in and adjudicate. 'The right to die' is the latest hot topic to be dropped into the laps of the nation's senior judges.

The religious right has never forgiven the U.S. Supreme Court for its 1973 decision in *Roe v. Wade* to allow a woman the right to have a legal abortion. So successful have they been in keeping their dissent alive that a visitor to America listening to the news on the radio or television could be forgiven for concluding that abortion was still illegal here!

It is virtually certain that the right to die movement will have to spend the next twenty years defending the modest gains it has made so far. Successful ballot initiatives like Oregon's Measure 16 will be opposed in the courts with claims of 'unconstitutionality', attacked in legislatures and either overturned or neutered, or negated by counter initiatives specifically criminalizing assisted suicide.

Social progress never comes easily in a democracy, especially one so wonderfully open and argumentative as America's. That is why Nina Clark's book is a pithy and valuable record of the political battles so far over voluntary, medically-hastened death. As Winston Churchill commented, unless we learn from history we are destined to repeat its mistakes.

Derek Humphry
Oregon, September, 1996

Acknowledgments

About half way through writing what was originally my doctoral dissertation, I recognized the hidden agenda which compelled me to choose physician aid-in-dying as the topic I would research for three years: the inevitability of death frightened me and studying it offered a way to reconcile the dying process.

In my post-manuscript moments, however, I would be remiss to assert that I am without fear and at peace with the fact that death remains a reality for all of us. Both of my maternal grandparents passed away during the time that this project was under way—my grandmother just as I was beginning, and my grandfather as I was finishing. Even though I had thoroughly saturated myself with death and dying issues and believed that in the process I had fought a sufficient battle with mortality, I found these losses difficult. Thus, in spite of and perhaps because of my discomfort with death I continue to strongly believe that we should be able to at least control the time and manner in which it occurs.

As I worked on this manuscript, numerous people have been helpful at different points. Warmest thanks are due to the members of my dissertation committee: Dr. William W. Lammers, Chair, Dr. Alison Dundes Renteln, and Dr. Phoebe S. Liebig, who were supportive and always challenged me to go "one step further." Special thanks to Alison, for help in accessing legal information and for her wonderful mentoring skills.

Additional thanks go to: the Hemlock Society Headquarters in Oregon, especially Ms. Lois Schafer, for many conversations and for being expeditious about supplying me with various written materials; Dr. Gary Johnson, Editor of *Politics and the Life Sciences*, for helping me to refine Chapter Five; Mr. Derek Humphry, for guidance through e-mail and for his own inspirational writings; the staff at Garland Publishing, Inc., especially Kristi Long, for help in pulling this manuscript together; the members of the Pasadena Senior Center for participating in the survey used in this study; and finally, my many friends and colleagues who were so encouraging throughout this whole process.

My mother and special friend, Roma Turoff, in offering much reassurance, was fond of telling me that "if it were that easy, we'd all do it." In many respects, she has traveled this journey with me, clipping articles and passing along other pertinent, miscellaneous information, keeping abreast of new developments within the movement, and enthusiastically engaging in verbal discourse. Everyone needs a cheerleader for endeavors such as this one. Fortunately for me, she was mine.

In counting my blessings, I consider Todd D. Clark, my husband and best buddy, one of my greatest. He has made many cups of tea and coffee, lent me his good humor when mine was nowhere to be found, and in spite of his own extremely demanding schedule, willingly shared his computer and statistical expertise with me, in addition to facilitating the creation of tables and figures. Many thanks, Todd, for ardently pursuing your own goals and achieving your own success because in the process, you inspired me to strive for my own.

Dr. Nina Clark
Connecticut, October 1996

The Politics of Physician Assisted Suicide

I

Introduction

The way a society collectively interprets death and dying is critical for it is in this way that other important decisions, (e.g., health care and patient autonomy) are addressed. Since we all commence with the knowledge that death is certain, it is essential some consensus be reached with respect to how this important phase of life is to be addressed. Some scholars suggest that we are a society so obsessed with death that we continue to deny that it is ever going to occur (Hoefler & Kamoie, 1994). The irony is that the process of "beginning," or being born, has been appropriately studied and perfected whereas the manner in which individuals make their grand "finale" has been largely avoided. As such, patient self-determination and the question of whether individuals have the fundamental right to hasten their own death continue to be unresolved and greatly debated issues.

As the quest for longevity continues, the assumption is that many wish to live beyond the natural life span of seventy to eighty years. Modern medical technology (e.g., respirators, cardiac resuscitation, artificial feeding and hydration, and drug treatment) makes it technically possible to keep a person "alive" and delay dying. Unfortunately, what technology has been unable to assure is quality of life. No longer capable of caring for one's basic needs, patients are often forced to forfeit their dignity by having to rely on either an artificial mechanism or another person. Consequently, living life becomes burdensome and humiliating since inherent in the notion of living is the guarantee that certain personal freedoms will be protected. Severe illness, however, categorically precludes individuals from making even the smallest decisions (such as when to eat dinner) and from carrying out the most mundane of activities (such as using

3

the restroom). In part, it is the freedom to make these decisions and to engage in such activities which gives each person autonomy. When this is no longer possible, a "quick" exit becomes a viable option, if not a welcome relief. Respected by some and condemned by others, these individuals who eventually make the decision to seek aid-in-dying are compelled to do so in a furtive manner since to date assisted suicide is not legal in any state.[1]

The 1990s, however, have witnessed some efforts (including advance directives, the durable power of attorney, the do-not-resuscitate order, and the Patient Self-Determination Act) aimed at the expansion of individual liberty and patient autonomy. Advance directives[2] do not, however, allow individuals the latitude of avoiding the final stages of terminal illness by requesting aid-in-dying. While advance directives serve the function of allowing an individual to prepare for a "worst case" scenario, they do not offer a practical way to ameliorate end-of-life suffering or a painful, humiliating death. In November, 1992, Californians had a chance to express their views, as they cast their votes on Proposition 161, The California Death With Dignity Act. Co-authored by attorneys Robert Risely and Michael White, the measure was a refined version of Washington state's Proposition 119, which sought to do what had not yet been done: legalize assisted death and affirm that it is a fundamental right.

The underlying premise appeared to be simple enough at first glance: in the event that mental and physical suffering should progress to such a degree as to limit the quality of life, there should be some manner of hastening one's own death. After all, proponents argued, this would not only be for the benefit of the ailing patient, but also for those having to watch the continual deterioration of their loved one. In addition, it would serve the nation's universal objective of trying to contain health costs, since keeping a person alive by mechanical means or keeping them comfortable while he/she is dying is typically quite expensive.

The opponents, however, could not and did not see any form of "suicide"[3] as a simple matter and much of their efforts focused on how the medical profession and particularly the elderly population would be adversely affected if Proposition 161 had passed. When Oregon voters passed Measure 16, which championed the right of terminally ill patients to request physician aid-in-dying, in November, 1994,[4] the opposition was heard loud and clear. Opponents asserted that suicide is an abhorrent act and to suggest that a physician take part in such activity is in direct conflict with the traditional role of a physician, which is to heal and to cure. In addition, the primary objective of the medical profession is to give rather than take life. The argument that allowing someone to choose to die would be more "economical" was dismissed as generally inconsequential since so many other facets of the issue (for example, the value of human life) were much more compelling than the fiscal aspect.

PURPOSE OF STUDY

Several lines of inquiry will be addressed:

1. examine the different ways in which the American political system has responded to the issue of patient autonomy;
2. explore its viability as an object of direct democracy;
3. study the political activity and attitudes of individuals in relation to physician assisted suicide, particularly the elderly, since they are "disproportionately affected" by end of life issues (Glick, 1991; p. 304); and
4. determine what role, if any, aging interest groups played in the "Yes" and "No" on Proposition 161 campaigns and assess future prospects and possible strategies.[5]

At the outset, I acknowledge a sympathy in favor of physician assisted death, citing the right of privacy as the primary constitutional vehicle to justify for its legalization. This work includes a case study of the path physician assisted suicide has taken with particular attention to Proposition 161, exploring activity in the courts, legislatures and past direct democracy efforts, with the issue history and analysis providing a framework. I argue that since the courts have been hesitant in affirming active voluntary euthanasia, the people have taken it upon themselves to create a proposed law and have used the initiative process to expedite its passage. It is purely by default that physician assisted suicide has ended up as an object of direct democracy. At no point in time was it determined that the initiative process would yield *better*, only *quicker* results (as Chapter Four will discuss), since the traditional policy-making institutions seemed to be at an impasse. Thus, it follows that if the American political system or legislatures had been successful in expanding patient autonomy in this manner, direct democracy efforts would have been unnecessary.

The conceptual framework for this study centers around what I have chosen to call the Default Model. This Model operates on three assumptions:

1. The formal political institutions, such as the courts and legislatures, have "failed" to promulgate some type of coherent policy regarding physician assisted suicide.
2. A certain segment of the public is "restless" for action on a particular issue (here physician assisted suicide).
3. Assisted suicide has become a ballot issue for the same reason that the courts and legislatures have been unable to affirm its constitutionality: the difficulty of resolving the inherent moral and ethical dimension of the subject.

Issues such as physician assisted suicide end up being matters of "personal choice" and are thus private. The arguments on both sides of the debate are so strong that to take a stand one way or the other often creates an intense controversy. In support of this point, Glick and Hays (1991) suggest that the right-to-die issue is similar to abortion since both concern the preservation of life, albeit at opposite ends of the life cycle. Consequently, institutions, interest groups and individuals as well sometimes refrain from being decisive in support of, or in opposition to, physician assisted suicide in an effort to avoid offending anyone and to avoid heated controversy and/or debate.

One of the arguments to be developed in this study is that the right to seek aid-in-dying is indeed protected by the constitutional rights of privacy and self-determination. Although the right of privacy is not absolute, landmark cases such as *Griswold v. Connecticut* (1965) and *Roe v. Wade* (1973) offer precedents which established that individuals do possess the prerogative of personal autonomy, which falls within the realm of the right of privacy. Recognizing the conflict of privacy and public (state) concerns, physician assisted suicide is a concept that decidedly favors the terminally ill individual, since it is the patient and not the "state" who would have to endure the suffering precipitated by a terminal illness.

THE PRIMARY ISSUE

The right-to-die movement in the United States began with the founding of the Euthanasia Society of America in 1938 and has grown rapidly since that time, primarily due to the life-prolonging power of medical technology. Glick (1992) traces the movement's 50-year history from the early 1940s to the present, covering major national and state-level legislative and judicial events, as well as the often acrimonious conflict between various interest groups. In 1976, the same year that *In re Quinlan* case was decided, California enacted the first Natural Death Act. Since that time 48 states have passed legislation or developed judicial policy on withdrawal or withholding of treatment in hopeless cases, but with little uniformity (Glick, 1992). This diversity is partly due to the wide array of definitions used: euthanasia (voluntary active, passive, involuntary active); assisted suicide, aid-in-dying, physician-assisted death/suicide; end-of-life decision making; do not resuscitate codes; patient self-determination; and right-to-die (Carpenter, 1993).

Acts of euthanasia are classified as active or passive and voluntary or involuntary.[6] Passive euthanasia, withholding treatment and allowing the patient to die, is regarded as permissible (Rachels, 1989), but direct action intended to kill the patient (active euthanasia), such as lethal injection, is not.[7] This view is firmly supported by the American Medical Association, which speaks approvingly of ceasing to use extraordinary means in certain cases (e.g., medicines, treatments and operations which offer a reasonable hope of recovery) (Sullivan, 1989: 57). Voluntary acts require the consent by either the patient or the patient's family (Pletcher, 1992).

Still, the distinction necessitates further clarification. The label active euthanasia is applied if the action is aimed at producing death, if termination of life is sought, chosen or planned (by the patient), and if the intention is deadly (Sullivan, 1989: 57). In contrast, the underlying intent present in a voluntary passive euthanasia case is to avoid prolonged suffering by the patient. On December 4, 1973, the House Delegates of the American Medical Association adopted the following statement:

> The intentional termination of the life of one human
> being by another--mercy killing--is contrary to that
> for which the medical profession stands and is
> contrary to the policy of the American Medical
> Association.
>
> The cessation of the employment of
> extraordinary means to prolong the life of the body
> when there is irrefutable evidence that biological
> death is imminent is the decision of the patient
> and/or his immediate family. The advice and
> judgment of the physician should be freely available
> to the patient and/or his immediate family (Rachels,
> 1989: 45).

Later, in 1982, the AMA went one step further, announcing for the
first time that it was ethical for physicians to withdraw or withhold life
supports from hopelessly ill patients (Glick, 1990: 78). By 1984, a
small group of physicians proposed a bill of rights for the dying,
advocating that emergency resuscitation and intensive care should be
in line with the wishes of the patient and family (Logue, 1993). In
many ways, these actions sanctioned passive euthanasia which
continues to be widely accepted by the medical profession.
Additionally, there are published accounts which suggest that active
euthanasia does take place. "It's Over, Debbie," anonymously
submitted to and printed by the *Journal of the American Medical
Association* in 1988, described how a gynecology resident relieved a
twenty-year-old dying cancer patient by injecting her with twenty
milligrams of morphine. This story garnered much criticism because it
was viewed as an abuse of professional power. If it is the physician's
responsibility to see to it that the patient is as comfortable as possible,
even though the drugs already being administered appeared to be
ineffective, perhaps the most "humane" action was in fact to expedite
"Debbie's" death.[8]

Upon learning about this story, some members of the medical
profession were appalled, asserting that such activity "violates one of
the first and most hallowed canons of the medical ethic: doctors must
not kill" (Gaylin, et al., 1989: 26). But even the most ardently opposed
physician will attest to the fact that there have been times when "the
best thing to do" in the case of a terminally ill patient has been

difficult to determine. What is professionally considered the right course of action, however, is not necessarily the most humane, although presumably as members of the medical profession, physicians always strive to operate in the most humanitarian fashion. In this case, the question is whether or not it was the doctor's intention to act in a humane manner. Rather, this was taken for granted and speculation largely focused upon what the most humane maneuver would have been (e.g., administering stronger doses of medication to Debbie in an effort to effectively control her pain). Would it have been more humane simply to allow Debbie to die a natural death? This lack of consensus as to what constitutes humane behavior on the part of medical professionals has intensified the controversy surrounding end-of-life treatment.

Realizing that the opportunity for cure is passed, a physician has two options: first, that of maintaining the life of a "dying" patient through the extremely difficult times of transition from active life to inactive life and from inactive life to death, or second, to withhold certain supportive measures which would enable nature to take her course more quickly (Koop, 1989: 75). Herein lies the dilemma. Is it humane for a physician to allow his/her patient to suffer the agony generally associated with a terminal illness simply because of the medical profession's blanket credo that doctors must give rather than take life? If, in fact, the physician in question decides to withhold life sustaining measures, he/she must make certain that such a wish has been enunciated in an advanced directive. It is considered homicide, punishable by imprisonment, if a physician acts on his/her own recognizance in the cessation of life sustaining treatment. In reality, it is the distinction between passive and active euthanasia which determines whether a physician has acted legally or illegally.

Even though the medical profession has not reached agreement on physician assisted suicide, what has the law done to encourage consensus and cohesion? Quite simply, while death and the prolongation of life as a consequence of medical technology have always been important legal questions (Berger, 1993; Shapiro & Speece, 1981), no decisive action has been taken in an effort to affirm patient autonomy to such an extent. Berger points out that the law knows it must deal with this issue as evidenced by the words of Justice Joseph Lumpkin in 1905:

> Death is unique. It is unlike aught else in its
> certainty and its incidents. A corpse in some respects
> is the strangest thing on earth. A man who but
> yesterday breathed and thought and walked among
> us has passed away. Something is gone. The body is
> left still and cold, and is all that is visible to the
> mortal eye of the man we knew. Around it cling love
> and memory. Beyond it may reach hope. It must be
> laid away. And the law--that rule of action which
> touches all human things--must touch this thing of
> death (*Louisville & N.R. Co. v. Wilson*, 1905).

Why then is there such a push for physicians to become
involved if there are such deep-seated ethical issues involved?
Specifically, why not completely take physicians out of the aid-in-
dying equation and allow family members and friends to help loved
ones to commit suicide? Hemlock Society[9] Founder, Derek Humphry,
posits that a corollary objective in relieving human suffering *via* active
euthanasia is to ensure that it is done in a dignified manner. When
individuals are forced to enlist the help of their friends and family
members furtively, lack of access to prescription medication means
that they have no choice but to employ methods which are generally
regarded as "second best" and are decidedly less dignified. Carbon
monoxide poisoning, cyanide poisoning, shooting and smothering are
decidedly less humane ways of encouraging death than drug overdose
or lethal injection because they take longer and are more painful. For
example, in the case of carbon monoxide, in addition to the fact that
death does not always come quickly, an agonizing headache often
ensues while the patient is conscious. Physicians, on the other hand,
would eradicate the need to resort to such drastic measures since their
access to medication is almost always ensured, making drug overdose
or lethal injection much more dignified and humane options.

Perhaps the issue of control is central to the dilemma. Typically,
the exact time of an individual's death has long been regarded as a bit
of a mystery. The "when your number is up, it's up" attitude seems to
have offered some comfort over the years, implying that the
burdensome decision of when one's life comes to an end is not one's
own. Many base their understanding of death on some type of religious
faith, specifically that it is the creator of humankind, God, who has the

liberty to take life, since it is God who first gave it. The belief in God as creator of human life is the foundation of this moral perspective. In religious dialogue, life is often discussed in terms of being a gift. Important to note, however, is the fact that the exact time of death is unknown is of comfort only to those who are healthy and want to remain living. But to those who are terminally ill, suffering the devastating effects of the disease, continuing to live becomes agonizing. Understandably, due to continual physical and/or mental deterioration, the good things in life become obscured and the decision of when one's life should end is no longer necessarily burdensome but rather is welcomed.

METHODOLOGY

The data for this study include multiple sources. At the outset, library research proved useful as it provided a comprehensive background on the issue and laid a solid foundation for further research. Primary sources of information included journals, both political and medical, newspaper articles, and books. Predictably, as election day grew closer, newspapers and weekly/monthly magazines provided the most in-depth coverage of Proposition 161 and the controversy surrounding it. A moderate amount of information was obtained from television programs and television/radio interviews. The end of the campaign witnessed unabashed attempts at persuasion on both sides most frequently in the form of radio and television advertisements.

Public opinion polls were useful for the purpose of witnessing how attitudes toward active euthanasia had changed over the years. Pre-election polls volunteering information about how the public at large was feeling about this issue were useful for predicting the outcome of the election and exit polls provided the "truth" about how the public had actually voted and offered valuable perspective into how pre-election support/opposition translated into votes.

Exactly one week before the November 3, 1992 election, a survey was conducted at the Pasadena Senior Center in Pasadena, California on October 28, 1992. One hundred thirty-eight individuals responded. The purpose of this survey was to gain some sense of how the senior population (those age 50+) would be voting on Proposition

161 and what their general feelings were regarding physician assisted suicide. It is important to note that the results are not representative of the elderly population as a whole since the population sampled was not randomly chosen. Instead, this group of senior citizens were selected with the knowledge that they comprised the "intellectual elite" of the Pasadena Senior Center population. The term "intellectual elite" is derived from the fact that these individuals were participants in an academic program titled "Senior Curriculum" which attracted only those who were willing to pay $140.00 for three eight-week quarters of academic instruction, thereby demonstrating their commitment to life-long learning. Out of the 2,500 members of the Pasadena Senior Center, roughly 200 joined Senior Curriculum. The main reason behind selecting this group of individuals is the assumption that they were the group *most likely* to have examined the issue and formed an opinion one week before the election. Thus, this survey is a case study.

The survey was one page in length. It was administered prior to the beginning of class and turned in at the end of the session. The first half contained all closed-ended questions which attempted to gauge voter awareness and to see if each individual had decided one way or the other how he/she was going to vote on Proposition 161. The second section primarily contained closed-ended questions with one open-ended question. The main purpose of this second half was to break down the respondents by demographic characteristics. For example, respondents were asked to indicate their gender, party affiliation, educational attainment, and religious affiliation. A Chi Square test of Association was then performed to determine if there was a correlation between the four variables and support of or opposition to the measure. The open-ended question invited criticism of Proposition 161 and this was useful in determining which aspects might impede passage of the Initiative. Finally, figures and tables were created in an effort to facilitate explanation and understanding of the data.

This study commences with a look in Chapter Two at the existing policy options concerning patient autonomy and the extent to which they have been effective. Next, Chapter Three addresses the courts and their activities regarding the right-to-die. Documented evidence as well as informal analysis lends plausible explanations for the judicial gridlock concerning the right-to-die. The conceptual framework for this study, the Default Model and how it relates to assisted suicide, is discussed in Chapter Four. In addition, the critical issues of "timing" and "gestation" are explored in the context of attempted legalization of an issue. Chapter Five examines the activism of the elderly population, both at the macro (interest group) and micro (individual) levels, employing the use of public opinion, pre-election and exit polls and independent analysis in addition to the survey conducted at the Pasadena Senior Center in October, 1992. Finally, Chapter Six provides an overview of the general findings, speculates on the future of physician assisted suicide as an initiative issue, and offers predictions and suggestions regarding legalization.

NOTES

[1]There are laws in thirty-six states prohibiting assisted suicide (Quill, 1993: 141). Other states simply do not have a law against it, but this does not mean that assisted suicide is legal.

[2]Advance directives will be discussed in greater detail in Chapter Two.

[3]While suicide is no longer "against the law," it is still considered morally unacceptable. One might conjecture that physician assisted suicide might be more likely to be legally and morally acceptable if the general act of suicide did not possess such a negative stigma.

[4]Oregon citizens voted 51-49 percent in favor of Measure 16.

[5]Although a comparative study would be both useful and interesting, the focus of this work will be on the United States.

[6]Dana Hirsch (1990) suggests that "the distinction between passive and active euthanasia is artificial and without merit. It is illogical to permit a doctor to withdraw life support systems without incurring a penalty, while imposing a penalty on a doctor who helps implement a patient's desire to end his suffering" (p. 842).

[7]For the purposes of this study, physician assisted suicide is referred to variously as active euthanasia, aid-in-dying, self-deliverance, physician assisted death, and voluntary active euthanasia.

[8]A 1994 poll of members of the New Hampshire Medical Society indicated that many believe that physicians should have the legal right to assist in a dying patient's suicide. Of the 47% who responded, 45% asserted that physicians should, at the patient's request, have the legal right to prescribe a lethal dose of a drug for a dying, mentally competent patient (Serrell, 9/18/94).

[9]In August, 1980, Derek Humphry and his second wife, Ann Wickett, formed the Hemlock Society, an organization "supporting the option of active voluntary euthanasia for the terminally ill" (Humphry, 1990: 116). Derek Humphry had a special interest in the mission of the organization since years earlier, in England, he had helped his first wife to die. For a full account, see *Jean's Way* (1978).

II

EARLY POLICY DEVELOPMENTS

Whether or not an individual is terminally ill or simply wishes to take precautionary measures when they are in good health, the extent to which he/she may extend their autonomy is the same. The reality is that individuals are not at liberty to ask for assistance in dying. Thus, if a person is terminally ill, he/she must continue to live until the disease finally takes its course. Life and death represent black and white scenarios. But what choices are present in the gray areas? Many are unsure. This chapter seeks to inform and educate the reader of present policy options.

An examination of what is currently available underscores the assertion that physician assisted suicide dares to push personal autonomy one step further and in doing so, challenges citizens and policy-makers to ascertain whether, due to universal vulnerability to terminal illnesses, existing policy options are sufficient to relieve suffering. The main objectives of this chapter are to: (a) consider existing right-to-die policy options; (b) address their strengths and limitations; (c) discuss how the elderly, in particular, have responded to these policy options; and (d) understand what these early right-to-die policy developments portend for physician assisted suicide.

HOSPICE CARE

According to physician assisted suicide opponents, hospice care, also known as comfort care or palliative care, provides a more compassionate, humane alternative. If an individual wishes to discontinue life-sustaining treatment, in effect, he/she is choosing to die and while there is nothing that can be done to hasten death (e.g., lethal injection or a drug overdose), the cessation of treatment will bring about this end. In such a case, those involved in the administration of comfort care will seek to keep the patient comfortable and relatively free from pain while the disease progresses to the point of death. Dame Cicely Saunders, the founder of the modern concept of hospice, asserts that hospice care offers a middle path between two undesirable approaches in caring for the terminally ill—high technology medicine or death by euthanasia (Campbell, Hare, & Matthews, 1995: 37). Other advocates suggest that hospice care allows individuals to assert their autonomy, since no heroic measures (including drugs or action which may arrest the condition or delay death) are taken. In addition, it is a dignified, humane approach since the individual is still permitted to choose death over disease and in doing so, to experience little or no pain.

While hospice may be a viable alternative to assisted suicide, there are several restricting factors. Specifically, what is often overlooked in considering this option is that unfortunately, there is a definite lack of available hospice beds and home care is often necessary.[1] Additionally, even though medication is administered while a person is under hospice care, the main objective being to keep the patient comfortable until he/she dies, at least ten percent of pain cannot be remedied (Girsh, 1992).[2] Moreover, as Dr. Timothy Quill suggests, if comfort care is to be considered an effective alternative, physicians must keep up with the new methods which have been developed for pain control (1993: 80). Often, this is not the case.[3] In fact, a survey of 1,400 doctors and nurses in five hospitals across the United States revealed that many physicians and nurses do not give dying patients enough drugs to relieve pain (*AARP Bulletin*, 2/93). Many hospice patients must continue to endure pain simply because their physicians are unaware of the most effective drugs or combination of drugs to ward off intense pain.

In addition, hospice care sometimes proves to be a financial burden. Comfort care is currently a Medicare benefit and some other insurers are finally beginning to include it (Quill, 1993). Thus, only those patients with proper insurance and a prognosis of less than six months to live are able to avail themselves of this option. The limiting factor is that the patient has to have someone at home who can serve as the primary caregiver and is responsible for the majority of care since hospice care often takes place at home (Quill, 1993). The caregiver is occasionally helped by professional and paraprofessional staff (Quill, 1993: 102). Thus, those who do not have a primary caregiver are often excluded. Patients on Medicare-certified hospice programs can sometimes be admitted to an inpatient hospice for symptom control, or to give their families some respite, but a limit of one to two weeks is generally imposed (Quill, 1993: 103).

What is also problematic is that when a physician decides to abandon measures designed to "cure" the patient, and shift to comfort care, insurers will often stop coverage because the hospitalization is no longer considered "acute" or necessary for improving the person's condition (Quill, 1993: 103). This sometimes has the effect of obliging the patient to continue unwanted, invasive, and expensive medical treatment in order to guarantee insurance coverage.

Most importantly, however, is that pain is not the only factor involved in the decision to die. The many indignities which accompany a given disease or simply the natural dying process may be what makes the individual decide to hasten his/her own death.[4] Hospice care entails dying relatively slowly as compared to assisted suicide, and this often means having to endure the many indignities of a certain disease for a lengthy period of time. Although the term "dignity" is frequently used in the course of every day conversation and is understood as unique to each individual, it also "involves the integration of a person's physical, emotional, intellectual, and spiritual aspects" (Quill, 1993: 104). Many would agree that this is the essence of one's being. It is possible to utilize elements of hospice care (i.e., pain and symptom management) up until the time when a person's quality of life, very directly related to an individual's feeling and perception of his/her own dignity, deteriorates to such a degree that the process of living is burdensome. At this point, aid-in-dying provides a dignified way of exiting an undignified life.

Also significant is that in traditional medical care increased suffering is reluctantly accepted as a side effect of treatment that is directed primarily at extending the patient's life (Quill, 1993: 78). In hospice care, "unintended shortening" of a patient's life is accepted as a potential side effect of treatment, just as long as the primary purpose is to relieve suffering (Quill, 1993: 78). In this way, albeit unintentionally, the effects of comfort care can and often do hasten death. Yet, this fact is often obscured and perhaps the main reason for this is that palliative care advocates would rather that the emphasis be on "comfort" rather than "death," even though death is frequently the anticipated result.

The "double effect" absolves physicians from responsibility for indirectly contributing to the patient's death, provided he/she intended only to alleviate the patient's symptoms (Quill, 1993: 78).[5] In many ways, this "double effect" has freed physicians so that they can effectively treat severe physical pain without being morally or legally accountable if that treatment unintentionally leads to an earlier death. The question of how one judges intent is compelling, which leads one in turn to wonder about the actual premise of hospice care. Does the "double effect" merely provide a loophole for those physicians who wish to aid a patient in dying? How would a determination be made after a patient dies if the physician's intent was to medicate the patient properly in an effort to relieve suffering or to invite death? Realistically, could not assisted suicide be considered "easing the passage" toward death, which also happens to be the basic credo of comfort care?

In fact, since the passage of Oregon's Measure 16 in November 1994, the question of how hospice care and assisted suicide will co-exist has arisen. For example, Derek Humphry described the relationship between hospice and the Hemlock Society as a "friendly alliance" (Campbell, Hare, & Matthews, 1994: 36). John A. Pridonhoff, Humphry's successor as Executive Director of the Hemlock Society, has asserted that the missions of hospice care and the Hemlock Society are not mutually exclusive and that hospice and Hemlock are already in "quiet" cooperative endeavor in the care of the terminally ill (Campbell, Hare, & Matthews, 1994: 36).

Aside from availing of hospice care, what measures are available to those who are terminally ill or who wish to take precautions before he/she becomes terminally ill? Moreover, how far has patient autonomy truly been extended to date? The following section explores other options for individuals wishing to address end-of-life issues prior to the onset of potential terminal illness.

ADVANCE DIRECTIVES:
THE LIVING WILL AND DURABLE POWER OF ATTORNEY

The Karen Ann Quinlan decision had a long-term affect on public opinion and the law regarding care for the terminally ill. Before 1975, right-to-die legislation had been introduced in only five states (Humphry & Wickett, 1990: 108). After Joseph Quinlan's request had first been denied by the Superior Court, and during the appeal to the Supreme Court, seventeen bills of this nature were introduced in different states (Humphry & Wickett, 1990: 108). None of them passed until California, frequently recognized as a trend-setting state, passed the California Natural Death Act in 1976. Although it was seriously flawed until it was changed in 1991, it recognized the right of a competent terminally ill patient to refuse medical treatment and to execute a directive stating his/her wishes (Girsh, 1992: 334). One year later, in 1977, fifty bills were introduced in thirty-eight states, and in Arkansas, Nevada, New Mexico, North Carolina, Oregon, and Texas, bills were signed into law sanctioning the use of living wills (Humphry & Wickett, 1990: 108). As of 1994, living wills exist in forty states (Quill, 1993: 190).

The living will and the durable power of attorney are known as "advance medical directives" and they first began to emerge in the late 1960s.[6] During this time, individuals who were concerned that they should not be forced to endure life-sustaining treatment wrote open letters to their families, friends, physicians, and clergy describing their wishes for treatment, or lack thereof, should they become terminally ill. These letters became known as "living wills" and at the time, were not intended as legally binding documents (Hill & Shirley, 1992: 14). The intent was to communicate preferences in an effort to preserve patient autonomy and to guide caregivers. Oftentimes, however, these living wills were ignored or disregarded by the caregivers. Additionally, it was up to the physician as to whether or not he/she wished to act in accordance with the patient's advance directive. Thus, in an effort to legitimize the status of living wills, states have not only passed laws sanctioning the use of advance medical directives but have also provided guidelines for preparation and specific circumstances when they can be used (Hill and Shirley, 1992: 14).

There are two types of living wills, each with a specific purpose. The first type defines a general philosophy of care that a patient would want should he/she lose mental capabilities (Quill, 1993: 191). For example, a person may wish to forego heroic treatment in the event that he/she is terminally ill and there is little or no chance of restoring the person's "quality of life" in addition to his/her life. Feeding tubes or other nutritional and hydration measures, may *not* be considered "heroic" and such intervention may very well be taken unless the patient has clearly specified that he/she does not wish to undergo such treatment. The second type of living will lists a series of specific interventions that a person might choose if he/she should become incompetent under several well-described circumstances (Quill, 1993: 191). These forms describe several patient scenarios in paragraph form, and then ask the respondent to check "yes" or "no" to a list of interventions of varying invasiveness and potential to prolong life (Quill, 1993: 191). Both of these living wills are effective to the extent that they offer a way for individuals to address end-of-life issues in a well-thought out manner.

There are, however, a few difficulties associated with living wills. For example, what course of action should be taken when the illness is similar to, but not the same as, the one described and responded to in the living will? Under current law, it is not acceptable to assume that medical professionals will simply administer the same/similar treatment if the condition is slightly different than the one addressed in the living will. This is understandably problematic since there is virtually no way to anticipate every type of illness and method of treatment.

Moreover, living wills require the individual to make decisions about interventions and treatments about which they may know little (Quill, 1993). A treatment which a person may deem "useless" or too painful may indeed have the intended effect of achieving an overall goal of getting better and restoring that person's quality of life. Once refusal of treatment is specified, however, the medical professional in charge is hesitant to go against the written wishes of the patient even if the treatment would be truly beneficial. Furthermore, in articulating one's wishes in a living will, it is often difficult to anticipate what type of invasive treatments may be administered or what heroic measures will be taken. Often, the average person does not possess the knowledge of the different types of medical procedures, making it difficult to assess the viability of such treatments in a crisis situation.

The limitations of living wills make it prudent to appoint a durable power of attorney for health care (also known as the Health Care Proxy) which evolved in an effort to further expand the rights of incompetent patients by granting competent adults the right to authorize someone to make decisions for them should he/she become unable to do so themselves. Again, the California legislature led the country by enacting the Durable Power of Attorney for Health Care Decisions Act in 1976. Specifically, this Act confers on another person (a health care "agent," of sorts) all the rights of a patient (Hill & Shirley, 1992). The job of the designated proxy is to help make informed decisions on the patient's behalf, using the patient's values and beliefs, not necessarily his/her own (Quill, 1993: 195). Consequently, many of the legal restrictions are avoided so that the rights of incompetent persons are affirmed. Most notable is the fact that it is decidedly a broad law which does not require that the patient be terminally ill for the agent to withdraw or refuse treatment (Girsh, 1992). In reality, the durable power of attorney allows the agent to respond on behalf of the patient to a specific situation which may not have been addressed in the person's living will. The one exception is artificial hydration and nutrition. In some states, an agent may be prohibited from refusing this treatment on behalf of an incompetent patient without demonstrating knowledge about the patient's specific wish (Quill, 1993: 196). This is somewhat easily avoided since every individual is free to indicate in a written directive whether or not he/she would like to be artificially fed and/or hydrated in an emergency situation.

Given the chance to articulate one's wishes and prepare for a "worst case scenario," why wouldn't more individuals complete a living will and a durable power of attorney? In fact, less than ten percent of the population has completed a living will or selected someone to serve as his/her health care agent (Quill, 1993: 196).[7] According to a study financed and made public in 1995 by the Robert Wood Johnson Foundation, half the patients who died in hospitals were in moderate to severe pain at least half the time, and more than one third of those who died spent at least ten days in intensive care, comatose or on a ventilator (Lewin, 6/2/96: A16). The fact is that there are barriers to the process of completing an advance directive. Specifically:

1. The fear of death often inhibits persons (especially the elderly) from taking such steps since signing a living will necessitates facing the inevitability of death, for which they are unprepared, even in later life. Moreover, as Hoefler and Kamoie (1993) suggest, Americans put much faith in medical technology and they tend to demand that the latest technology be used in every instance. This mind-set precludes them from facing up to tough choices.
2. The forms, always legalistic in nature, prove to be intimidating and difficult to understand.
3. There may be conflict within a family as to who should be appointed the health care agent. It is presumably "easier" not to confront such a decision than to create family dissension.
4. It is often hard to predict whether an emergency intervention will improve the person's quality of life or sentence him/her to a slow and painful death.

Just how effective are advance directives for the purpose of asserting patient autonomy? In spite of the fact that much of the literature supports the use and efficacy of advance directives, there is seemingly little information on how well they accomplish their intended purpose. In an effort to remedy this situation, Marion Danis and his colleagues conducted a two year prospective study in which 126 competent residents of a nursing home and 49 family members of incompetent patients were interviewed to determine their preferences with respect to hospitalization, intensive care, cardiopulmonary resuscitation, artificial ventilation, surgery, and tube feeding in the event of critical illness, terminal illness or permanent unconsciousness (Danis et al., 1991). The findings revealed that the effectiveness of written advanced directives is limited by inattention to them and by decisions to place priority on considerations other than the patient's autonomy (Danis et al., 1991). While the primary purpose of an advanced directive is to preserve patient autonomy, this study suggests that in caring for incapacitated patients, physicians balance respect for autonomy with other competing ethical principles in order to make what they believe are the wisest decisions (Danis et al., 1991).

Unfortunately, the physician's best judgment is frequently contrary to the wishes of the patient. Since the study was performed in only one nursing home, generalization of the results is hampered, but the conclusion does, however, point to the fact that advance directives do not always guarantee that the patient's wishes will be recognized and affirmed.

For example, a 1996 *New York Times* article (6/2/96: A1 & A28) offered a detailed account of Michigan resident Brenda Young, a thirty-eight year old woman, who is in need of complete care. In 1992, after suffering repeated seizures and on the advice of her physician, Brenda signed an advance directive and gave her mother power of attorney to stop treatment in the event that Brenda became unable to do so herself. After her next seizure, in spite of her mother's insistence that life support not be administered, Brenda was put on a ventilator, a feeding tube was inserted, and she was maintained through a two-month coma. In defending their actions, Brenda's physicians asserted that they were acting in her best interests and that they had no way of predicting how disabled she would be (Lewin, 1996).

Conversely, other scholars assert that advance directives succeed in accomplishing their intended purpose (Davidson et al., 1989). Specifically, in a study conducted on physicians' attitudes toward advance directives, the findings revealed that almost 80% felt positively about advance directives (Davidson et al., 1989). In fact, a majority of the physicians surveyed indicated that advance directives had indeed influenced treatment decisions in critical situations. In addition, of all the favorable arguments, those concerned with patient autonomy received the strongest support among the physicians, thereby supporting one of the primary purposes of these documents: that patient autonomy should be preserved.

In spite of the fact that physicians are generally in favor of advance directives, some physicians such as Timothy Quill (1993) and Diane Meier (1991) assert that living wills, for example, do not always serve the purpose of resolving end of life decisions.[8] Older patients, for instance, run the risk of not being explicit enough in articulating what type of treatment he/she would like continued/discontinued. In a similar way, new treatments may be developed between the times that the person signs the living will and becomes seriously ill. Moreover, the question of durability raises doubt about the efficacy of living wills. The fact that living wills are frequently written years in advance means that individuals may change their minds about decisions to forgo life-sustaining therapy. When a life-threatening situation eventually arises, the person's verbal wishes may or may not comply with what he/she had stipulated in writing years earlier.

While legalized assisted suicide would not mitigate the need for advance directives since living wills and the durable power of attorney enable individuals to articulate their desires in the event that they should become mentally incapacitated, it would certainly allow individuals to respond to the circumstances of the situation at the time. Furthermore, advance directives in no way provide total patient autonomy and the certainty that should being alive become too painful and/or humiliating due to terminal illness, hastening death would be a viable option and is a comforting thought. I acknowledge that advance directives and assisted death are not congruent notions or procedures. Physician assisted suicide would, however, provide the (critical) privilege of immediate rather than future decision-making.

In preparing for a "worst case scenario," individuals often opt to fill out a do-not-resuscitate (DNR) order. Not to be confused with advance directives, the following section seeks to delineate the differences between the two and also to address the strengths and limitations of the DNR order.

THE DO-NOT-RESUSCITATE (DNR) ORDER

Many barriers inhibit individuals from signing another type of end-of-life document, the do-not-resuscitate (DNR) order. The latter allows a person to indicate by way of written directive if and under what circumstances he/she wishes to be resuscitated. Important to note is that a DNR order is not the same as an advance directive for a few reasons. First, an advance directive only goes into effect in the future, if a person becomes incompetent; it does not address the type of care that he/she would want in the present or in the future if he/she remains competent and can be asked directly (Quill, 1993: 198). A DNR order specifically addresses cardiopulmonary resuscitation. Second, a DNR order covers only the "potential present or future use" of the latter, regardless of whether one is competent or incompetent (Quill, 1993: 198). In contrast, advance directives cover a broader range of decision-making for the future if a person loses his/her mental capacity (Quill, 1993: 198).

In spite of the argument that the DNR order is effective, a few difficulties inherent in the concept and its use render it less than satisfactory. For example, in accordance with current ideology and practice, hospital policies typically require that cardiopulmonary resuscitation be attempted unless a DNR order has been written (Hackler & Hiller, 1990). This is problematic because physicians are sometimes forced against their own judgment to revive a patient who is hopelessly ill and would not benefit from prolonged existence. In fact, the literature suggests that this often contributes to the patient's suffering and that rehabilitative efforts should not have even been attempted in the first place (Iverson, 1989; Hackler & Hiller, 1990; Gray et al, 1991). To date, there is no legislation that allows a physician to use his/her own judgment to determine whether or not the patient will benefit from resuscitation and to then act accordingly. If a patient has neglected to write a DNR request, family permission for the order must be obtained. When emotions are running high, due to the collapse of a loved one, it is frequently difficult to extract an objective response from that individual's relative. Some scholars (see Hackler and Hiller, 1990) advocate a change in policy so that physicians can write a DNR order over family objections when:

1. the patient lacks decision-making capabilities;
2. the burdens of treatment clearly outweigh the benefits;
3. the surrogate does not give an appropriate reason in terms of patient values, preferences, or best interests, and;
4. the physician has made serious efforts to communicate with the family and to mediate the disagreement (p. 1281).

Implicit in this notion is the idea that the legal duty of the physician and the hospital is to the patient only; there is no duty to the surrogate (Hackler & Hiller, 1990: 1283). Efforts at implementing such a policy have been unsuccessful presumably because of the potential for abuse on the part of medical professionals.

In addition, when treatment is needed outside of the hospital setting, at home or work, for example, and is administered by emergency medical service workers (e.g., paramedics), resuscitation is virtually always attempted (Iverson, 1989). There is often scant information with which to discriminate among the pre-hospital patients on whom resuscitation should be performed and sometimes the friend or family member of the incapacitated individual is unable to find the living will (Iverson, 1989) proving that he/she did not wish to be resuscitated. If an emergency service medical worker were to refrain from resuscitating a patient, a pre-hospital DNR order would have to be in existence. Currently, no jurisdiction has a formal provision for generalized pre-hospital DNR order (Iverson, 1989: 18). One of the main reasons for this is that such an order, completed outside of the hospital setting, would predictably invite even more abuse than an in-hospital directive. For example, it would be difficult to determine in an emergency situation who wrote the DNR order. Furthermore, without the specific legislative guidance and legal language, medical personnel would be uncertain about the legality of a pre-hospital DNR document (Iverson, 1989: 18) meaning that the DNR order could be a "fake" and the attending medical personnel may not even realize it.

It should be properly clarified that advance directives and the DNR order were adopted by individual state legislatures, rather than by the federal government. Consequently, not every state extends a uniform right of personal autonomy to its citizens. The following section discusses what action has been taken by the national government to uphold individual patient autonomy.

FEDERAL EFFORTS: THE PATIENT SELF-DETERMINATION ACT

At the federal level, the Patient Self-Determination Act (1990) signified an effort to ensure that individuals knew that they had the right to address end of life issues in the form of an advance directive. In addition, its enactment suggested that policy makers have affirmed that individuals should have some autonomy when it comes to terminal illness and the prolongation of life.[9] This Act mandates that upon admission to an institution such as a hospital or skilled nursing facility receiving Medicare or Medicaid funding, patients must be informed of their rights, under state law, to refuse medical and surgical treatment. The facility may not, however, require that the patient have an advance directive, but rather merely ask them if they already have one (Cotton, 1991). Upon learning that a patient has not prepared a directive prior to entering the hospital, the hospital gives the patient the opportunity to read and sign one.

At the outset of its implementation, the Patient Self-Determination Act was hailed as a crucial step in motivating patients to make advance decisions about end-of-life care. The Act, which took effect December 1, 1991, is recognized as the "medical *Miranda* warning" (Cotton, 1991). Undeniably, this federal law is revolutionary in that it is the first of its kind to acknowledge that every American does, indeed, possess a "right-to-die." However, actual implementation of the Act has been inconsistent (Warrick, 1993). According to State Department of Health Services lawyer, Marlys Huez, forty-five nursing homes--about one-third of them in Los Angeles County--have been cited for violations ranging from failure to provide community education to failure to notify patients of their rights under the law (Warrick, 1993: E8). In addition, state inspectors, who are charged with enforcement of the law, found that in some cases, nursing homes were blatantly ignoring patients' final wishes, administering cardiopulmonary resuscitation (CPR) (and practicing other life-sustaining treatments) to seriously ill and dying patients over their objections (Warrick, 1993: E1).

Another major criticism of the Patient Self-Determination Act is that the patient is informed of his/her right to complete an advance directive upon being admitted to a hospital when the patient may very well be incapable of making such serious decisions. If the individual is in severe pain, for example, it is unlikely that he/she will possess the capacity to comprehend the forms, reasonably assess his/her condition and then state his/her wishes in an articulate manner. Thus, the fact that the patient is being advised of such a right is immaterial if he/she does not possess the faculties required to complete the process.

Lastly, compliance with the law can be achieved by merely having a clerk ask if the patient has completed an advance directive, recording the answer and then handing the patient several additional forms in the packet of admitting information (Quill, 1993). This is unlikely to initiate the complex dialogue and thought processes that are required to complete an advance directive in an informed manner (Quill, 1993).[10] What is disappointing is the fact that although the action is taking place and the law is being fulfilled, the desired intent is not being achieved.

For the Patient Self-Determination Act to be truly effective, perhaps it is the physicians and not the admitting clerks who need to be informing patients that their patient rights can be expressed in the form of an advance directive. This would achieve two things: it would give the patient the option of addressing and discussing end-of-life issues in a circumspect manner in their physician's office when he/she is not suffering from the effects of a given disease/condition; and the true intent of the Act would be being fulfilled. The senior population would greatly benefit from a physician/patient consultation since seniors may, at some time or another, require further explanation about the purpose of filling out an advance directive, the forms, and his/her individual health history and condition(s).

In line with one of the objectives of this study, to determine how the elderly population in particular feel about right-to-die issues, the next section explores their knowledge, attitudes and behavior regarding advance directives.[11]

THE ELDERLY POPULATION: KNOWLEDGE, ATTITUDES AND BEHAVIOR

In an effort to understand the attitudes and behavior of the elderly population with respect to advance directives, I employ the use of a study conducted by Elizabeth Gamble and her colleagues in North Carolina in 1990. A questionnaire was administered to seventy-five ambulatory elderly persons between the ages of sixty and eighty years of age by personal interview at community dining sites in Pitt County, North Carolina, a semi-rural eastern county with a population of approximately 100,000. The questionnaire consisted of nineteen questions concerning perceived status of personal health, knowledge of the North Carolina Right to Natural Death Act and interpretation of the document, treatment preferences in terminal care, desire to discuss the subject with a physician or other person, and attitudes toward such a discussion.

The results were noteworthy in the following ways:
- Fifty-two percent of the individuals indicated that they were familiar with living wills.
- In spite of this, none of the persons interviewed had signed a living will and only three percent responded

affirmatively when asked if they had discussed a living will with their physicians, although eighty-one percent stated the desire to discuss end-of-life care with their physicians.

- The majority of the elderly persons in this study wanted their medical care limited in the event of a terminal illness.[12]
- In support of this, eighty-six percent stated the desire to receive basic medical care or comfort care only.

Gamble and her colleagues acknowledge that these findings are flawed to the extent that they are not representative of the elderly population as a whole and therefore discourage making generalizations. Given the fact that no studies had been done at the time on the acceptance of living wills by an elderly population (Gamble et al., 1991), the findings do offer the possibility of speculation and insight into the attitudes, beliefs and knowledge of the rest of the senior population.

What do these results suggest about physician assisted suicide? Three points emerge: (1) the elderly population do have an interest in addressing end-of-life issues; (2) the fact that eighty-six percent of those surveyed wished to only receive comfort care, avoiding invasive, heroic measures suggests that perhaps they may not be willing to endure the mental and physical deterioration associated with a terminal illness and; (3) given that the elderly population in this study expressed the desire to have their medical care limited, attitudes toward physician assisted suicide are positive rather than negative.

Given the documented evidence that while advance directives are desired by much of the public as a means of furthering patient autonomy and have, in fact, been adopted by forty states (Quill, 1993), the question of whether physician assisted suicide will follow a similar path is explored next.

ONE STEP FURTHER: PHYSICIAN ASSISTED SUICIDE

Perhaps one of the main reasons why assisted suicide engenders so much confusion is because it is a matter of social regulation. Specifically, according to Tatalovich and Danes, *what* is being regulated is not an economic transition but a social relationship, defined by community values, moral codes, and norms of personal conduct (1988: 2). In this way, social regulation provokes intense, persistent controversies (Tatalovich & Danes, 1988: 3). By this definition, physician assisted suicide and right-to-die issues in general, can be considered matters of social regulation, since values, morals, and norms of personal conduct are clearly central elements and it is to be expected that significant debate would ensue.

Tatalovich and Danes further assert that courts promote legal change in social regulatory policy by asserting individual rights and liberties against traditional social values (1988: 214). Courts provide a mechanism for promoting legal changes in social regulations that are beyond the immediate control of the political leadership (Tatalovich & Danes, 1988: 214). When the latter statement is applied to the right-to-die, it is indeed true that the courts have been instrumental in furthering patient autonomy, as in the *Quinlan* case. But the fact is that the courts have been and continue to be hesitant in meeting the public demand for complete and total patient autonomy (e.g., physician aid-in-dying).

While the courts have certainly confronted the issue, their decisions have been less than consistent because of the conflict between private versus state interests and the difficult question of whether the right of privacy truly encompasses the right to hasten one's own death and ask for assistance in doing so. As I will show, the legal system has not been an effective mechanism to date in furthering patient autonomy in this manner and to such a thorough extent. Court decisions involving active euthanasia have been inconsistent. The only element which has remained consistent is that no court has ever affirmed this right.

The courts have, at different times, examined euthanasia (both passive and active) as a privacy issue. They have succeeded in determining that a person has the legal right to refuse medical treatment, even if it means that death is the inevitable result. It is true that written directives have certainly extended personal liberty in this area to some degree, but these written directives do not allow a mentally competent person who is terminally ill to deliberately choose death over life. Although assisted suicide even with the victim's consent is considered homicide, the courts have continued to hedge in being decisive as to the length and type of punitive action.

The next chapter examines how the courts have approached passive and active euthanasia cases in an effort to provide a solid foundation for exactly why physician assisted suicide has become an object of direct democracy.

NOTES

[1]According to Hill and Shirley (1992), a complication in hospice care and planning has been the dramatic impact of the AIDS epidemic. As the demand for long-term, palliative care for persons in the terminal stage of AIDS has increased, many hospice programs have opened their doors to people with AIDS, even though the patients often do not meet the formal requirements for admission, due to the unpredictable nature of the illness (p.73). In an effort to contribute to the fight against the virus, many patients are being treated with experimental drugs, even as they seek palliative care in the final stages of their illness. Hospices are increasingly willing to allow the use of aggressive or experimental treatments in cases where such treatments offer the possibility of reversing, not simply managing, the life-threatening symptoms of the disease.

[2]A corollary argument advanced by Daniel Callahan (1987) asks the question of whether the possibility of controlling a patient's pain justifies prolonging his/her life in an otherwise hopeless illness.

[3]Dr. Quill acknowledges that even if death is the only way to relieve a patient's suffering, a physician cannot intentionally facilitate death. By maintaining this artificial distinction, the medical profession undermines the true intent of comfort care: to help people maintain their dignity, control, and comfort all the way through the final phase of their illness until death (1993: 108).

[4]Important to note is that comfort care does not guarantee that death will come easily, without mental and physical suffering. Its goal is to keep the patient *as comfortable as possible*, which may not be significant enough to eradicate end-of-life suffering.

[5]See also Glanville Williams *The Sanctity of Life and the Criminal Law* (1957).

[6]According to Henry Glick, while California enacted the nation's first living will law in 1976, the Florida legislature was the first to consider the right-to-die in 1968.

[7]A recent study revealed that some form of an advance directive was desired by ninety-three percent of the patient population that was surveyed (Quill, 1993).

[8]See *Death And Dignity* (1993) by Dr. Timothy Quill and "The Physician's Experience" by Dr. Diane Meier, *The Mount Sinai Journal of Medicine* (5 October 1991).

[9]Glick asserts that like most other medical issues, the right-to-die has been mainly a state political phenomenon. The Patient Self-Determination Act represents one of the first attempts of federal recognition of the issue.

[10]Other studies suggest that while physicians seem to be favorably disposed to advance directives, they are hesitant to initiate discussion about them (Gamble et al., 1991).

[11]In exploring the attitudes, knowledge and behavior of the elderly population, I do not intend to imply that age can and should be used to *predict* specific preferences regarding end-of-life treatment. But given the fact that human beings are often more prone to serious illness in the later stages of life, examining the attitudes of the elderly is both useful and interesting.

[12]Although none of these individuals had signed a living will, three potential barriers to signing a living will were identified: lack of knowledge; lack of communication between physicians and their patients; and a preference for proxy decision-making by a family member (Gamble et al., 1991).

III

Court Responses

The courts serve as an excellent point of departure for explaining why citizens have come to see the initiative process as an effective means of articulating their need and desire for legalization of physician assisted suicide. This chapter will primarily focus on how the courts have responded to past cases of passive and active euthanasia. It seeks to address the right of privacy or self-determination in the context of physician assisted suicide and also to explore how it has been applied in the past to (other) issues of personal autonomy. In addition, specific cases will be discussed in an effort to demonstrate how courts have wrestled with these challenging constitutional matters.

I assert that court decisions involving cases of (passive and active) euthanasia have been largely inconsistent. Therefore, it is difficult to depict any trends in judicial thinking about this topic. One scholar suggests that "the courts, rather than protect, only confuse the issue" [assisted suicide] (Humphry, 1990: 220). Much of the "confusion" has had to do with the fact that there are two established legal categories into which euthanasia may fit: homicide and suicide.

For example, in England, up until 1961, attempted suicide or death which resulted from a suicide attempt was illegal (Barrington, 1990). In fact, prior to 1961, those persons who did not succeed in their suicide attempt could be arrested and criminally prosecuted. Even though the act of attempting suicide or succeeding was eventually decriminalized, assisting suicides was not. In fact, active mercy killing is still universally classified as homicide, even with the victim's consent (Sherlock, 1992: 553). Specifically, S2(1) of the 1961 Suicide Act states: "A person who aids, abets, counsels or procures the suicide of another, or an attempt by another to commit suicide, shall be liable

35

on conviction on indictment to imprisonment for a term not exceeding 14 years" (Barrington, 1990).

In spite of the fact that active euthanasia is considered homicide even with the victim's consent, the courts have come to different conclusions as to the length and type of punitive action. Each case appears to be judged on a case by case/*ad hoc* basis, that is, if prosecution even ensues. Numerous accounts cited by Derek Humphry[1] describe how persons who have aided in suicide have not had to serve time in prison because it was determined that they had already undergone sufficient punishment from the stress associated with such activity. Often, the charge was reduced. The whole notion of assisted suicide being considered a homicidal act is problematic to the proponents of the euthanasia movement since the basic underlying premise of assisted suicide is, above all else, mercy and not malice[2]. Furthermore, when carrying out a wish of a patient by withdrawing life-sustaining treatment, this action presumably is not considered murder. Instead, it is viewed as the implementation of the patient's constitutional rights of self-determination and privacy (Berger, 1990: 137), which will be discussed in this chapter.

When assisted suicide is considered an act of homicide, the underlying intent in complying with the terminal patient's wishes becomes obliterated. Even though the objective is to alleviate a loved one's suffering, the person who assists has to be prepared to endure some suffering of his/her own by eventually having to face criminal charges in a court of law. Thus, it is not surprising that there are a growing number of cases of "secret" or "concealed" suicide assistance (Schaffer, 1986). At the same time, attempting to decide the intent with which a person assisted in a suicide is difficult and is often just beyond the scope of the legal system[3]. The courts do, however, still engage in speculation as to the true motive of an assisted suicide and this in part has encouraged confusion regarding the constitutionality of assisted suicide and has consequently led to inconsistent decision-making.

Some scholars suggest that the courts have created an exception to the common law rule. Specifically, the fact that individuals are sometimes not prosecuted or convicted after having aided in a suicide perhaps implies that the courts are attempting not to recognize euthanasia as a criminal act (Berger, 1990). Even when authorities take the rare step of charging physicians with murder for intentionally carrying out the wishes of a patient's family (and without compliance with a state's living will statute to disconnect equipment and discontinue treatment to prolong the life of a patient), the judicial trend seems to be for the courts not to sustain the charges (Berger, 1990: 137). Thus, the fact that the courts are increasingly willing to refrain from applying the homicide label to euthanasia means that they may be leaning toward active euthanasia as a guaranteed right and that some type of legal mandate which offers consistent immunity or a set of guidelines for those who assist in suicides is badly needed. In the absence of such legislation, the ultimate decision as to whether each particular case is a homicidal act may be dependent upon the mood of the court at that time.

What is the distinction between murder and helping someone to commit suicide? In the eyes of the court, interest largely centers around avoiding irrational self-destruction.[4] It seems to be generally accepted that actual participation in a suicide, shooting a willing victim for example, as opposed to facilitating or aiding the act, is murder (Schaffer, 1981: 351).[5] There is no jurisdiction in the United States which recognizes consent to homicide (Schaffer, 1986: 351).[6] Certain states have however enacted a "Natural Death Act," which provides a living will form that a person may use to declare that, in the event of a terminal illness, life-sustaining treatment should not be administered.[7] These statutes absolve from criminal liability health professionals and hospitals which obey the living will (Schaffer, 1986: 354). Following a patient's wishes in this way is not considered murder or helping a person to commit suicide.[8]

According to the *Quinlan* (1976) decision, a passive euthanasia case, although withdrawal of life sustaining procedures from a patient whose vital processes were maintained by a mechanical respirator would accelerate death, the ensuing death would not be "homicide," but rather expiration from existing natural causes. Most interesting is the fact that in this same decision, the Court specifically stated:

> Constitutional protection from criminal prosecution where death is accelerated by termination of medical treatment pursuant to right of privacy extends to third parties whose action is necessary to effectuate the exercise of that right where the patients themselves would not be subject to prosecution or the

> third parties are charged as accessories to an act
> which could not be a crime (*In re Quinlan*, 1976:
> 15).

Thus, while immunity is granted to the individual who "pulls the plug," those administering an overdose of a certain drug, with the intent of inducing death, are still criminally liable.

Judicial hesitancy in affirming the right of individuals to assist in suicides and in promulgating regulatory guidelines, has created a continuing and predictable cycle of events. Health care facilities are largely unwilling to discontinue treatment in the absence of a written directive, in an effort to avoid issues of intent and liability. Even if a written directive does actually exist, there may still be confusion regarding its legitimacy.[9] Consequently, friends or family members of the patient in question are forced to enlist the help of the courts to sanction removal of any life sustaining mechanism. As the courts continue to refrain from setting a precedent, the scenario is repeated the next time a friend or family member of a terminally ill individual either seeks removal of a life supporting instrument or aid-in-dying. The next sections will examine court activity and the elements impeding court progress in ruling consistently on this matter. The discussion initially turns to the right of privacy, a concept which is at the heart of the right-to-die debate.

IS THERE A CONSTITUTIONAL RIGHT-TO-DIE?

The right-to-die is not explicitly enumerated in the United States Constitution. There is, however, a right of privacy, which can be gleaned from certain constitutional amendments and which can also be interpreted as the right of self-determination. Also known as the "right to be let alone," this concept was applied in *Griswold v. Connecticut* (1965) and further affirmed in *Roe v. Wade* (1973). In *Roe*, the U.S. Supreme Court interpreted the First, Fourth, Fifth and Fourteenth Amendments in the Bill of Rights as creating the right.[10] Specifically, the right of privacy emanates from the "penumbras" or "shadows" cast by the contents of these amendments and articles. It was in *Quinlan* (1976), a passive euthanasia case, that the New Jersey Supreme Court held that the right of privacy encompasses the right to refuse medical treatment even if the result is death. While the right of privacy was at one time not a basic liberty, contemporary Americans have incorporated this right into their lives and make many of their life decisions based on the guarantee of the right of privacy/self-determination (e.g., whether or not to employ the use of birth control devices). Similarly, it can be argued that the value of a person's life is not lessened by an individual's decision to decline treatment but by the refusal to permit a competent adult the right of choice.

One of the most frequently cited statements of the right to control one's body is from *Union Pacific Railroad v. Botsford* (1891), a case in which the Supreme Court refused to order a personal injury plaintiff to undergo a pretrial medical examination. The Supreme Court stated the following:

> No right is held more sacred, or is more carefully guarded, by the common law, than the right of every individual to the possession and control of his own person, free from restraint or interference of others, unless by clear and unquestionable authority of law (*Union Pacific Railroad v. Botsford*, 1891).

Proponents of the right-to-die claim that physician assisted suicide involves a personal right of privacy/right of self-determination. They argue that since it has been affirmed that the right of privacy is congruent with the right of self-determination, whether or not one wishes to endure the suffering generally associated with terminal illness becomes a personal decision. The opposition, however, counters that this is not a decision which only affects the terminally ill individual and is therefore not solely a privacy issue. Rather, the lives of children, family, and friends, in addition to the life of the person aiding in the suicide, are affected by such decisions.

How have the courts responded to the privacy issue in relation to passive euthanasia? The specifics of the *Quinlan* case, which led to the Court's ultimate decision, demonstrate just how far the Court went in extending patient autonomy and the right of self-determination. Karen Ann Quinlan was a 21-year-old girl who lapsed into a coma after her friends found that she was not breathing. She was subsequently placed on a respirator. After having been on a respirator for three months, Karen's father, Joseph Quinlan signed a release to permit physicians to turn it off. The physicians in charge of Karen, however, refused to comply with Mr. and Mrs. Quinlan's wishes. Consequently, the parents were forced to solicit the help of the courts, with the hope that Mr. Quinlan would be appointed Karen's guardian. If the courts were willing to appoint Mr. Quinlan as Karen's guardian, he would have the express power of authorizing discontinued use of all extraordinary means of sustaining her life. The judge, however, ruled in favor of the hospital since Karen did not meet the Harvard criteria for brain death.[11] The court disputed the right of privacy and cited the State's interest in preserving the sanctity of human life.

The Quinlans appealed this decision to the New Jersey Supreme Court, which eventually overturned the lower court's ruling in an effort to affirm Karen's right of privacy stating that "a patient's right to privacy was greater than the State's interest in the preservation and sanctity of human life" (*In re Quinlan*, 1976: 13.). So certain was the New Jersey Supreme Court that the patient's interest outweighed those of the state, that it wrote:

> We have no hesitancy in deciding . . . that no external compelling interest of the State could compel Karen to endure the unendurable, only to vegetate a few measurable months with no realistic possibility of returning to any semblance of cognitive or sapient life. *(In re Quinlan*, 1976: 39)

In addressing the right of privacy, the Court relied on *Griswold v. Connecticut* and stated,

> the right of privacy is broad enough to encompass a patient's decision to decline medical treatment under certain circumstances, in much the same way as it is broad enough to encompass a woman's decision to terminate pregnancy under certain conditions (*In re Quinlan*, 1976: 40).

Thus, insisting that Karen remain in a vegetative state would have been violating what the Court determined was her Constitutional right. Moreover, the fact that she was in a vegetative state did not mean that this right was nullified since Karen was technically still alive. The only way to prevent destruction of her right of privacy was to permit her family to make the decision. When a third party is permitted to venture a best guess at what the wishes of the patient would have been had he/she been conscious, this is known as "substituted judgment." Even though Karen was weaned from the respirator just as her parents had wished, she did not die. Instead she remained living in a coma fed through tubes, until she died almost ten years later, in July, 1985. Her parents never petitioned the court to have the nutrition/hydration tube removed.

This case was clearly influential in future decisions of this nature. In fact, the *Quinlan* decision is cited more than any other case by all other courts (Glick, 1990: 79). But it is important to keep in mind that this expansion of patient autonomy was a state rather than federal supreme court decision. When the U.S. Supreme Court confronted this issue in *Cruzan* (1990), it did not affirm the opinion of the New Jersey Supreme Court. Instead, as will be discussed, it chose not to interpret the right of privacy as broadly as did the New Jersey Supreme Court.

The courts have, on balance, been consistent in applying the rights of privacy/self-determination to cases of informed consent[12] wherein prior to agreeing to any treatment, an individual must be given information about the treatment (Berger, 1990; Humphry, 1990). According to this doctrine, it is essential for a physician to obtain consent from a patient before commencing any treatment procedure. The patient must be provided with explicit information as to what the procedure will entail, an assessment of any anticipated recovery or procedural difficulties, and alternative methods of treatment. Based upon all of the information given to the patient, he/she can either choose to refuse or undergo the procedure.[13]

While this is entirely permissible regarding the right to refuse medical treatment even if death results, the right-to-die, *per se* is not and has never been recognized. If a patient refuses medical treatment and death ensues, the Court accepts this as an inevitable outcome. The Court is seemingly unwilling, however, to grant an individual the constitutional right to actively pursue his/her own death by lethal injection, for example, even though it has ceased to consider the act of suicide as a (punishable) crime. The Court's hesitancy in making assisted suicide a guaranteed right has to do, in part, with the fact that it asserts that it has a fundamental interest in protecting state concerns, some of which are considered utilitarian. They are delineated as follows:[14]

1. *Preservation of society.* The state has a legitimate interest in promoting a thriving and productive population. Allowing people to kill themselves legally or to assist in killing someone else runs counter to this interest. Furthermore, the patient who refuses life-saving treatment harms the community by depriving it of a productive member (Matthews, 1987). This last point, however, can be challenged on the ground that compelling individuals to realize their potential for "usefulness" is at odds with the ideal of individual freedom that guides American jurisprudence (Matthews, 1987: 730). It seems unreasonable that every patient who is contemplating refusal of treatment or aid-in-dying is still able to benefit society, especially since seriously ill persons inevitably become limited in their physical and/or mental capabilities.

2. *Sanctity of life.* This concept often is considered the foundation of a free society. By denying an individual the right to choose death, the courts believe that they may be promoting a general respect for life. This interest often overrides an individual's desire to hasten his/her own death. If individual autonomy and self-determination are themselves essential parts of what makes life valuable, then respect for the sanctity of life would be negated by refusing to respect a patient's refusal (Matthews, 1987). Reasonably, the state interest is strong when the patient can be restored to a qualitatively rich life and diminishes when the patient is terminally ill or severely disabled (Matthews, 1987: 731).

3. *Public morals.* The rejection of life-sustaining treatment is regarded as a form of suicide which conflicts with the general tenets of the Judeo-Christian culture, which believes only a divinity can control the cessation of life. The term public morals refers specifically to the "immorality" of self-destruction, an act which has in past years been a common revulsion to members of western culture (Cantor, 1983). According to Cantor, suicide, however, is no longer considered either "legally or popularly, as inherently immoral" (1973: 246).

4. *Protection of third parties.* The courts seek to protect three additional main interests which warrant consideration:

   a. Surviving Adults. The death of a relative or close friend may provoke grief, despair or other emotional harm in the surviving person. The inherent paternalism of the state is the motivating factor in attempting to minimize this type of trauma. Arguably, a variety of actions by a loved one, aside from death, may inflict emotional harm upon a loved one, such as divorce, physical or mental abuse, yet no court would suggest a legal order which would compel individuals to be nice to a friend or relative (Cantor, 1973).

   b. Physicians. In assisting in suicide or withholding treatment, physicians may be forced to act against their professional judgment. In addition, in complying with a patient's wishes, there is subsequent risk of criminal liability. Both sides of the argument have their merits. On the one hand, it is understandably difficult for a physician who is dedicated to the preservation of life to allow a "salvageable" patient to die. On the other hand, it is the patient and not the physician who is having to endure the emotional despair and physical limitations often associated with terminal illness.

   c. Surviving Minors. Where minors are present, safeguarding a child's welfare through the doctrine of *parens patriae* (the state's assuming the protective role of parent or guardian), may override a parent's objection to medical treatment (Cantor, 1973). When the parent is kept alive, the state assumes that the child continues to benefit emotionally and financially. This point can be challenged on two levels: it assumes that the child was emotionally and financially secure before the parent was taken ill; and that prolongation of the patient's life will guarantee continued emotional and financial security. Depending on the seriousness of the patient's condition and his/her financial circumstances before illness, this may or may not be true.

In protecting these basic human interests, as articulated by the state, the courts must find some legal justification for legalizing physician assisted suicide. As is the case with many relatively contemporary issues, such as abortion and gay rights, the Bill of Rights is devoid of any mention of such rights. Presumably, when the Constitution was being written, there was little way of forecasting that issues such as physician assisted suicide would arise, challenging the tenets of the personal limits they had sought to extend. One could certainly assert that the first ten amendments support the contention that the Framers intended to incorporate personal freedoms into this document in an effort to render the fundamental laws of the land enduring and resilient. Still, it is a dilemma as to exactly how far to extend personal autonomy and at the same time continue to protect the interests of all involved.

Thus, review of a landmark U.S. Supreme Court decision is necessary to understand and explain judicial difficulty and hesitancy in affirming personal liberty to such an extent by legalizing physician assisted suicide. It will become clear that the courts are reluctant to clarify individual autonomy with respect to the right-to-die.

THE U.S. SUPREME COURT: ACTIVITY AND OPINION

The case of Nancy Cruzan involved requested removal of life-support mechanisms, artificial feeding and hydration equipment. On January 22, 1983, Nancy Cruzan lost control of her car and was discovered lying face down in a ditch without detectable respiratory or cardiac function. In spite of this, her breathing and heartbeat were restored at the site of the accident. Nancy remained in a coma for approximately three weeks and then progressed to an unconscious state. Even though she was able to ingest some nutrition, surgeons implanted a gastrostomy feeding and hydration tube in Nancy with the consent of her husband.

After Nancy had been artificially fed and hydrated for nearly five years, her parents, Lester and Joyce Cruzan, petitioned the Court to allow removal of the life-sustaining mechanisms. A state trial court ordered removal of the nutrition/hydration tubes. But when the case was taken to the Missouri Supreme Court, it ruled against the Cruzans stating that there was not "clear and convincing" proof of Nancy

Cruzan's desire to have hydration and nutrition withdrawn. Instead, the Supreme Court chose to balance Nancy's interest against the State's interest in preserving life, concluding that the State's interest was strong in situations such as this, where the patient was not terminally ill (*Cruzan v. Harmon*, 1988: 419). The Court specifically stated:

> Given the fact that Nancy is alive and that the burdens of her treatment are not excessive for her, we do not believe that her right to refuse treatment, whether that right proceeds from a constitutional right of privacy or a common law right to refuse treatment, outweighs the immense, clear fact of life in which the state maintains a vital interest (*Cruzan v. Harmon*, 1988: 424).

The Court further elaborated that the state's living will laws did not extend to withdrawal of hydration and nutrition, a point which was not relevant to this case, given the fact that Nancy had never written an advance directive. She had only verbally communicated during the course of casual conversation to her friends that she would not want to continue to live in the absence of a "halfway normal" life (*Cruzan v. Harmon*, 1988: 424). The Court determined that this was not clear and convincing proof and unlike the *Quinlan* case, Nancy's parents were not permitted to make the decision for her.

Nancy Cruzan's case was taken to the U.S. Supreme Court where the decision was upheld. The Court went on to affirm that the State did not have to permit family decision-making in a situation such as this, even though Lester and Joyce Cruzan were presumably capable of doing so (*Cruzan v. Director, Missouri Dept. of Health*, 1990). While the state Supreme Court recognized that an individual does, indeed, possess a right to refuse treatment, as embodied in the common law doctrine of informed consent, the High Court questioned its applicability in this case due to the lack of clear and convincing evidence. Furthermore, it also refrained from recognizing a broad right of privacy, which would have supported an unrestricted right to refuse treatment, and even went so far as to express doubt that the U.S. Constitution embodied such a right (*Cruzan v. Director, Missouri Dept. of Health*, 1990: 2843).

Eventually, the clear and convincing legal standard was satisfied due to the efforts of family and friends, who collected and presented evidence of Nancy's true wish never to remain in a persistent vegetative state. In December 1990, a Missouri court finally ruled that Nancy's feeding tube could then be removed, and she died approximately ten days later, on December 26, 1990 at thirty-three years of age.

The long term effect of this decision is that states were, and still are, permitted to adopt whatever standards they see fit. This decision was not all that surprising given the conservative orientation of the Supreme Court during the 1980's and into the early 1990's. The conservative members on the Court continually seek to narrow the scope of individual decision-making (e.g., *Webster v. Reproductive Health Services*, 1989). In the same way that these conservative members chose to limit the availability of abortions, they chose to assert that unless an individual had executed an advance directive, his/her right of privacy could not be assured or guaranteed by having a guardian make the decision. In fact, Chief Justice Rehnquist argued that the State has wide discretion to assert the standards of proof necessary for determining the patient's wishes. In this way, the Missouri Supreme Court was not remiss in suggesting that before an individual's family can act in a surrogate capacity, the state must see "clear and convincing proof" that such an action would be in compliance with the patient's wishes.

The discrepancy in the court decisions of *Quinlan* and *Cruzan* is indicative of the contemporary dilemma--the absence of uniform standards. Although, similar in circumstances, but taking place in different states and at different times, the cases were not even judged according to the same standards. It is this inconsistency which prevents the members of the general populace from trusting that were they to be in a similar situation, their right of privacy/self-determination would automatically be applied, allowing for removal of artificial life-sustaining apparatus. The fact that the Courts have vacillated for years in deciding these cases is further proof that direct democracy efforts will ultimately be responsible for legalization and/or regulation of assisted suicide.

The cases reviewed have shared two common elements: the patients involved were not terminally ill (defined as having been given six months or less to live), although the quality of their lives was realistically minimal; and the decisions involved passive instead of active euthanasia. Have the courts been particularly lenient or strict when the individual in question is not terminally ill but still enjoys a certain quality of life? More importantly, how critical is the stipulation that the patient be "terminal?" Does the fact that the patient is conscious, thereby labeling this "brand" of euthanasia "active voluntary" make a difference? These questions are the focus of the following section.

THE CASE OF ELIZABETH BOUVIA

In 1983, Elizabeth Bouvia, a quadriplegic since birth, took her case to court in an effort to obtain permission to be allowed to starve to death while staying at Riverside General Hospital in California.[15] Her request was denied by Superior Court Judge, John H. Hewes, who affirmed that she had the right to kill herself, but "not with the assistance of society" (Beyette, 1992: E1). On appeal, the California Supreme Court affirmed the lower court's ruling and consequently, Bouvia went to Tijuana, Mexico to carry out her plan. Finding that the hospital was unwilling to cooperate and she checked into a motel, intending to enlist the help of her friends. Later, she abandoned this plan realizing that this would leave her friends in precarious legal and ethical situations.[16]

By 1985, Bouvia was forced to enter County-USC Medical Center for treatment of severe, persistent pain. Two months later, she was moved to a rehabilitative facility since she no longer needed acute care. At this point, she re-launched her campaign to die, asking that the artificial feeding tube be removed. The request was denied, but was overturned by a California state appeals court, which asserted that all patients, regardless of age, condition or motive, have the right to control their treatment. This was a huge step forward for the right-to-die movement.

But by the time of the decision, Ms. Bouvia was addicted to the morphine that controlled (and continues to do so) the pain caused by muscle spasms, scoliosis, arthritis, and osteoporosis. Even though she has repeatedly stated "I'd rather be dead than live like this" (Beyette, 1992: E1), Ms. Bouvia has chosen not to pursue her own death.

On August 14, 1996, I had a conversation with Ms. Bouvia's attorney and friend, Griffith Thomas, J.D., M.D. Dr. Thomas explained that Ms. Bouvia currently lives alone in an apartment in Southern California with round-the-clock attendants. She is essentially happy, is looking forward to writing a book in the near future and has given up the idea of dying.

Ms. Bouvia's case is complicated by a number of factors. Specifically, she won the right, as a non terminal, competent individual to refuse artificial feeding/hydration, but not to have physicians or other members of the medical staff to physically assist her in dying (e.g., by administering a drug overdose). This right, according to the court, is protected as an aspect of the constitutional right of privacy. Additionally, Ms. Bouvia's condition is not classified as terminal, since she does not only have six months or less in which to live. Rather, she has already survived ten years since her first request to starve to death and may, in fact, survive another ten, according to her doctors. This fact alone would preclude her from seeking a physician's help in dying.

That the courts encountered some difficulty in granting Elizabeth Bouvia the right to refuse medical treatment is somewhat understandable. In examining her quality of life, it must have seemed that Elizabeth Bouvia has lead a relatively fulfilling life. Even though she is quadriplegic, Ms. Bouvia has earned a degree from San Diego State University, been married (albeit for a brief amount of time), had become pregnant and then suffered a miscarriage and currently, she even smokes, which may serve as testimony to the fact that she has been able to "enjoy" some parts of her life. She also is in complete possession of her mental faculties, which enables her to be intellectually active. Thus, her physical immobility does not impair other important aspects of her life.

Although Elizabeth Bouvia's case was certainly important in right-to-die decision-making, even if a right-to-die initiative (Proposition 161), had passed Ms. Bouvia would not legally have been able to take advantage of the provisions simply because she is not by definition terminally ill. Propositions 119, 161 and Measure 16 called for assisted suicide with the stipulation that the patient be terminally ill. Moreover, advance directives were not useful to her in hastening her own death, simply because she was mentally alert, and her life did not necessarily need to be sustained by artificial mechanisms. Of notable importance is that Ms. Bouvia was able to eat and drink on her own. The fact that she was being artificially fed was purely the result of not wanting to eat and drink. Furthermore, after having fought so long and hard to be granted the right to hasten her own death, Ms. Bouvia ultimately decided against doing so. Did her efforts represent depression and frustration with her life at that time? Elizabeth Bouvia's case lends support to the opponents of assisted suicide who assert that legalization would be dangerous because depression causes individuals to seek death as an outlet, but that once the depression lifts, the will to live is ultimately triumphant.

OTHER ACTIVE EUTHANASIA CASES

In other cases where the courts have had to rule on cases of active euthanasia, the right of privacy has frequently been affirmed. The case of *Satz v. Perlmutter* (1978), involved Abe Perlmutter, a competent seventy-year old retired cab driver, who tried to remove the respirator which was sustaining his life. He suffered from amyotrophic lateral sclerosis (known as Lou Gehrig's disease or A.L.S.) and his physicians did not expect him to live more than a few hours without the respirator, although his life expectancy while he was on it was determined to be two years. The Florida Medical Center refused to honor his wishes, even though his family agreed with his decision. Because the Medical Center refused to cooperate, Mr. Perlmutter was forced to petition the circuit court for an order restraining the hospital from continuing his life-sustaining treatment.

Declaring that the patient was competent and was indeed entitled to enforce his constitutional right of privacy, the circuit judge issued the restraining order. Specifically, he stated that,

> Abe Perlmutter, in exercise of his right to privacy, may remain in defendant hospital, free of the mechanical respirator now attached to his body, and all defendants and their staffs are refrained from interfering with plaintiff's decision (*Satz v. Perlmutter*, 1978: 194).

The hospital appealed, and the Fourth District Court of Appeals basically concurred, holding that a competent patient has a constitutional right of privacy to refuse life-sustaining treatment after the prognosis of an agonizing terminal illness (*Satz v. Perlmutter*, 1978). Referring to the prolongation of Mr. Perlmutter's life, the court stated:

> . . . It is all very convenient to insist on continuing Mr. Perlmutter's life so that there can be no question of foul play, no resulting civil liability and no possible trespass on medical ethics. However, it is quite another matter to do so at the patient's sole expense and against his competent will, thus inflicting never ending physical torture on his body until the inevitable, but artificially suspended, moment of death. Such a course of conduct invades the patient's constitutional right of privacy, removes his freedom of choice and invades his right to self-determination (*Satz v. Perlmutter*, 1978: 164).

Mr. Perlmutter eventually died on October 6, 1978, when his respirator was disconnected.

Approximately one year after Mr. Perlmutter's death, the Supreme Court of Florida held that only intentional death raises the state's interest in preventing suicide (Humphry & Wickett, 1990: 245). Basically, the court equated disconnecting the respirator with refusing surgery (Humphry & Wickett, 1990: 245). Thus, while this case was important in that it upheld the rights of a competent patient to refuse continuation of life-sustaining treatment, active pursuit of death was not, and still is not permitted. What is problematic is that refusing surgery is regarded as "passive" even though an individual may know and may even intend for death to occur. This being true, the question remains if refusal of surgery should be considered "active" in the same way that requesting an intentional drug overdose is considered "active" euthanasia.

California was given the chance to decide a similar case in 1984. In *Bartling v. Glendale Adventist Medical Center*, seventy-year-old William Bartling was suffering from a minimum of four potentially fatal diseases, including lung cancer. Tubes were inserted into Mr. Bartling's chest and through his nasal passage and throat in order to re-inflate his lung. The lung did not re-inflate due to a hole made by the biopsy needle and he was placed on antibiotics to encourage healing of the punctured lung while a tracheotomy was performed and he was placed on a ventilator. Bartling was described as distressed and uncomfortable while on the respirator and after having asked to have it taken away, tried to remove it himself. In an effort to keep Mr. Bartling from attempting to remove the respirator, his hands were tied to the bed.

This case differs significantly from others in that Bartling was competent and had signed a living will which stated in part: "If at such time the situation should arise in which there is not reasonable expectation of my recovery from extreme physical or mental disability, I direct that I be allowed to die and not be kept alive by medications, artificial means or heroic measures" (1984: 220). Attached to the living will was a declaration from Bartling stating:

> While I have no wish to die, I find intolerable the living conditions forced upon me by my deteriorating lungs, heart and blood vessel systems, and find intolerable my being continuously connected to this ventilator, which sustains my every breath and my life for the past six and one-half (6 1/2) weeks. Therefore, I wish this Court to order that the sustaining of my respiration by this mechanical device violates my constitutional right, is contrary to my every wish, and constitutes a battery upon my person. I fully understand that my request to have the ventilator removed and discontinued, which I have frequently made to my wife and to my doctors, will very likely cause respiratory failure and ultimately lead to my death. I am willing to accept that risk rather than to continue to burden of this artificial existence which I find unbearable, degrading and dehumanizing. I also suffer a great deal of pain and discomfort because of being confined to bed, being on this ventilator, and from the other problems which are occurring (*Bartling*, 1984: 220).

In addition, not only had Bartling executed a Durable Power of Attorney for Health Care wherein he had appointed his wife as his attorney-in-fact, but Mr. and Mrs. Bartling and their daughter, Heather, had all signed documents in which they released Glendale Adventist and its doctors from any claim of civil liability in the event that they chose to honor Bartling's wishes.

In spite of the clear evidence demonstrating Bartling's wishes to avoid life sustaining measures, his treating physicians refused to remove the ventilator and/or the restraints which prohibited Bartling from removing the ventilator himself. Interestingly, past cases have taken issue with the notion of competency, arguing that the patient was not mentally competent and revocation of life sustaining treatment was unconstitutional. In this case, however, Bartling's verbal and written statements were positive proof of his mental competency.

The trial court held that the right to have life-support withdrawn was limited to comatose, terminally ill patients. While Bartling was not comatose, his lung cancer could certainly have qualified him as terminally ill. The court also concluded that as long as there was some potential for restoring Bartling to a "cognitive, sapient life," it would be inappropriate to issue an injunction (*Bartling v. Superior Court*, 1984: 220).

When the case was appealed, the lower court decision was overturned, stating that to deny Mr. Bartling's request to have the respirator removed was a breach of his right-to-privacy. Furthermore, because the patient periodically vacillated between wanting to live and wanting to die, did not mean that his decision making abilities were impaired to the point of legal incompetence (*Bartling v. Glendale Adventist*, 1984). Mr. Bartling's right to refuse medical treatment was found to outweigh any other interest of the state and/or medical profession. Specifically, the Court ruled, "If the right of the patient to self-determination as to his own medical treatment is to have any meaning at all, it must be paramount to the interests of the patient's hospital and doctors." (1984: 225).[17] Equally important, the Court indicated that a non terminally ill adult patient has a constitutionally based right to refuse and/or to terminate medical treatment. Even though Mr. Bartling ultimately won the right to have the respirator removed, he died before the court decided the case in his favor.

What is most troubling about this case is the fact that Mr. Bartling had gone about making his wishes known in what was and is generally considered the proper and acceptable manner. Although this case is over ten years old, it lends further support to the claim by some scholars and medical professionals that "enforcement of advance directives is (sometimes) not uniform" (Warrick, 1993: E1). Legalization of assisted suicide, while it may suffer the same "confusion" or occasional lack of uniformity as advance directives, would affirm the rights of an individual to "choose" death. Additionally, the right to request (both written and verbal) a lethal injection before an individual progressed into a comatose state would negate any possibility of medical professionals being "unsure" of the patient's true wishes.

Once again, while this case is important in that it did, indeed, affirm an individual's right to refuse life-sustaining treatment, thereby hastening one's own death, it was not recognized by the courts as active euthanasia. The difficulty seems to be with the words "active" and "passive." It appears that if the court determines that the action would be "passive," meaning that some type of life support mechanism is removed, it is construed as a humane action. Actively seeking aid-in-dying even when an individual is not on life supporting mechanisms, but does not want to have to suffer the last stages of their terminal illness, is a crime presumably because the court does not see pain and suffering as intolerable. Moreover, what is called into question is whether the right of privacy encompasses an individual's right to request someone else (e.g., a physician) to assist him/her in dying.

When individuals have aided in suicides, the prospect of prosecution has not been absolute even though assisting in suicide continues to be illegal. Conversely, there have been cases in which individuals aiding in a suicide have had to face the law. In 1920, for example, in the case of *People v. Roberts*, Mr. Roberts' wife had been enduring terrible pain resulting from multiple sclerosis.[18] She had unsuccessfully attempted suicide by herself and began to plead with her husband to help her die. Mr. Roberts eventually complied with her request and placed poisoned water on a chair next to her. After drinking the water, she died. Mr. Roberts was convicted of first degree murder, in spite of the fact that he had merely acted upon his wife's wish to die and that ultimately, it was she who hastened her own death by drinking the poisoned water. The fact that he had only enabled her to commit suicide, rather than actually killing her himself, did not mitigate his sentence.

The 1986 case of *Gilbert v. State of Florida* again demonstrates that the courts have not taken a more "lenient" stance when addressing cases of mercy killing.[19] Roswell Gilbert's wife, Emily, was a victim of both Alzheimer's disease and osteoporosis. Suffering from the combined effects of both diseases, she had in fact stated on occasion that her pain was so acute that she wished to die. Intending to relieve his wife of her plight, he loaded his gun and shot her in the head. He was prosecuted and later convicted. The Florida Court of Appeals affirmed the first-degree murder conviction noting that there was no evidence of a "mercy will" and the fact that Mr. Gilbert's intentions were purely altruistic were not meaningful to the court.[20] Mr. Gilbert was then sentenced to life in prison. However, four years later, he was granted clemency by Florida Governor Bob Martinez based on the fact that Gilbert was eighty-one years old and in poor health (Daar, 1995).

In 1996, when George Delury, a New York resident and former editor of *The World Almanac*, helped his fifty-two year old wife, Myrna Lebov, who suffered from Multiple Sclerosis to die by giving her a lethal cocktail, his motive came under scrutiny. Mr. Delury kept a diary in which he at one point wrote, "You are sucking my life out of me like a vampire and nobody cares. In fact, it would appear that I am about to cast in the role of the villain because I no longer believe in you" (Belluck, 1996: B26), thereby suggesting that he was at least partly motivated by self-interest. He pleaded guilty to a lesser charge of second degree attempted manslaughter on March 15, 1996, and served a six month prison term on Rikers Island.

There were a couple of other complicating factors involved in this case aside from Mr. Delury's motive. First, Myrna Lebov was not technically terminally ill. Secondly, not only did Mr. Delury's diary raise questions about his motive, but also about whether Myrna Lebov really wanted to die. Furthermore, Myrna Lebov's sister maintained that she had been coerced by Mr. Delury into killing herself.

There seems to be something very sinister in the eyes of the court in allowing a physician or friends/family members to access medication intended for overdose or to avail of other means in enticing death. To date, the courts have not expanded the right of privacy/self-determination this far. The fact of the matter is, however, that if a person is a quadriplegic, for example, and happens to be terminally ill and wishes to die, he/she is physically incapable of committing suicide. At this point, the help of another person becomes absolutely necessary.

Moreover, at the crux of the debate is the basic question of whether or not a terminally ill individual has a fundamental right to a humane and dignified death. If a terminally ill patient wishes to die, the options that are available are generally not humane and dignified. The *Gilbert* case is a perfect example. Roswell Gilbert possibly had no other means of hastening his wife's death other than to shoot her. Arguably, lethal injection and drug overdose are the "best" methods to hasten death. Specifically, when a lethal injection is administered, the individual usually lapses into a deep state of unconsciousness, there is no agonizing pain for the person receiving it and it is more bearable for the family members who are either assisting or who happen to find the individual. The same is true for drug overdose, barring any complications. In both cases, the person who has either ingested the medication or received the injection, usually lapses into a deep state of unconsciousness and then dies within minutes. In the absence of being able to obtain a sufficient amount of drugs or the lethal injection, individuals are often forced to seek death in undignified ways.

While individuals are permitted to sign advance medical directives indicating under what circumstances they do not wish to be kept alive, the durable power of attorney and do-not-resuscitate order do not seem to be "enough" in an age when AIDS and other (terminal) illnesses guarantee extreme physical and emotional deterioration. Consequently, the push for legalized physician assisted suicide comes from the desire to do more than just take precautions should one fall into a coma or need to be resuscitated and from the belief that active euthanasia should be considered a part of the right of self-determination.

Toward this end, there has been unprecedented activity in the courts since 1994. What follows is a description of the cases and their outcomes.

IN PURSUIT OF LEGALIZATION

Retired Pathologist, Dr. Jack Kevorkian, dubbed "Dr. Death" by the media, has been the focus of much media attention. Beginning in June, 1990, he helped a woman named Janet Adkins take her life with the aid of a "suicide machine," a mechanism designed by Dr. Kevorkian. Ms. Adkins was suffering from the early stages of Alzheimer's disease. She had sought experimental pharmacological treatment, which had failed, and had decided that she did not wish to live a life of progressive cognitive degeneration. In Adkin's estimation, her quality of life had become greatly diminished and she wished to spare not only herself, but her family and friends, the agony of the mental and physical deterioration associated with Alzheimer's. She had heard about Dr. Kevorkian and since she was a firm advocate of the right-to-die, arranged to fly to Michigan to seek his assistance (Warrick, 1992). After a single dinner conversation, he agreed to help her to die, and in an effort to avoid the legal ramifications of their actions, they decided that the actual procedure would take place in the woods, in the back of Kevorkian's old Volkswagen van.

While this was hardly the first case of active euthanasia *via* physician assisted suicide, it was one that captured the attention of the general populace and inspired much activism, both for and against aid-in-dying. Many had strong feelings against the actions of Dr. Kevorkian, asserting that he had abused his privilege as a medical professional. Others applauded his willingness to act to protect what he believed was a fundamental constitutional right, the right-to-die with dignity. Interestingly, a third of the persons he has helped to end their own lives have been age 65 and older (Leinbach, 1993).

The confusion about Kevorkian's actions largely centered around the question of whether it is within the line of duty for a physician to hasten death. The absence of a state law barring suicide assistance was the single most decisive factor when a Michigan judge threw out a murder charge that had been filed against Kevorkian (*New York Times*, 7/22/92: A6).

When murder charges were again brought against Kevorkian, they were also eventually dropped since a Michigan court determined that prosecution would be unconstitutional because the state still had no law against assisted suicide (*New York Times*, 1992).[21] He went on to assist in more deaths in Michigan and elsewhere, bringing the total number of suicides he has assisted in to forty one as of September 1996.

Originally, the cases were dismissed because an Oakland County Circuit Court ruled that the women had killed themselves and that Michigan had no law against assisted suicide. Trial judge, David Breck, wrote that "the act of assisting a suicide is not a criminal act," and added that "a person should have the right to insist on treatment which will cause death" (Lessenberry, 3/11/96: A13). But three years later, in December 1994, the Michigan Supreme Court ruled that assisted suicide had always been a "common-law crime," or one that was based on custom rather than legislation (Lessenberry, 5/15/96: A14). The case was then reopened.

Ultimately, prosecution did ensue and since 1994, Kevorkian has stood trial three times for providing aid-in-dying. All have resulted in acquittals. On May, 2, 1994, Dr. Kevorkian was acquitted of murdering Thomas Hyde, a thirty-year-old man suffering from Lou Gehrig's disease (Pasternack, 1994: A1). The jury agreed that Kevorkian's only motive in helping Hyde to die in August 1993 was to ease his suffering, as opposed to openly killing him (Pasternack, 1994: A1). Just about two years later, on May 14, 1996, a jury found Kevorkian not guilty of violating Michigan's common law against assisted suicide when he helped fifty-eight-year-old Marjorie Wantz and forty-three-year-old Sherry Miller, to die on October 23,1991. Interviews with members of the jury indicated that the prosecution had failed to prove beyond a reasonable doubt that Kevorkian had violated common law (Lessenberry, 5/15/96). Furthermore, jurors said they believed that the women themselves had made the decision to die based on videotapes the two women created describing their misery.

After the acquittal, Kevorkian's attorney, Geoffrey Fieger, predicted that "this will be the last Kevorkian trial" (Lessenberry, 5/15/96: A14). Michael Modelski, a former Oakland County assistant prosecutor who is a Kevorkian opponent, agreed that he probably will not be tried again for assisting in a suicide. As of August 1996, prosecutors have not filed charges against him in connection with the last deaths he has attended.[22]

While these decisions only invalidate the law and do not go so far as to actually make it possible for terminally ill individuals to request aid-in-dying in Michigan, like the decision absolving

Kevorkian of guilt, it is useful for the purpose of asserting that individual rights outweigh the state's interest. This could be the critical first step toward complete expansion of patient autonomy.

THE NINTH AND SECOND CIRCUIT COURTS OF APPEALS

In December, 1994, three individuals, four physicians, and Compassion In Dying, a Washington based non-profit organization incorporated in April 1993, which offers counseling and emotional support to terminally ill patients, filed suit against the state of Washington for declaring that the statute on promoting suicide violated the United States Constitution.[23] Chief Judge Barbara Rothstein of the United States District Court for the Western District of Washington, had originally struck down Washington's law barring physician assisted suicide on the grounds that it "deprives terminally ill patients of personal liberty guaranteed under the 14th Amendment" (Conner, 1994: A7). The state appealed and in *Compassion in Dying v. State of Washington*, the Ninth Circuit Court of Appeals ruled by a vote of two to one that: (1) the statute did not deprive persons seeking physicians assisted suicide or constitutionally protected liberty interest, and (2) facial invalidation[24] of the statue was unwarranted (49 F.3d 586). The majority opinion held that the Washington statute was necessary to protect the sick and the elderly and to keep physicians from becoming killers.

One year later, sitting *en banc*, the U.S. Court of Appeals for the Ninth Circuit, reversed the earlier ruling and determined by a vote of eight to three that the Washington state statute making it a felony to aid another person in committing suicide was unconstitutional as applied to physician assisted suicide. This time, the Court affirmed the earlier ruling of Chief Judge Barbara Rothstein--that the Washington statute violated the "liberty interest" of the Fourteenth Amendment.

The appellate rulings have far-reaching implications. While the Ninth Circuit's decision nullifies only the Washington statute prohibiting physician assisted suicide, also included in its jurisdiction are Alaska, Arizona, California, Hawaii, Idaho, Montana, Nevada and Oregon. The legal principles articulated by the Court of Appeals are the law of the entire circuit until there is a ruling by the United States

Supreme Court which is contradictory. There is wide speculation that the High Court is the next stop for this issue.

Currently, Oregon's Measure 16 is before the Courts. A permanent injunction was issued by U.S. District Judge Michael Hogan on the day before Measure 16 was to go into effect in the case of *Gary Lee v. Oregon*. He held that Measure 16 violates the equal protection clause of the Fourteenth Amendment by depriving persons who are terminally ill with six months or less to live of the protection of laws. Specifically, Judge Hogan referred to laws which intend to prevent suicide, such as the law providing for the involuntary commitment of persons who are clinically depressed and the law which makes it a crime to aid another person in committing suicide. Judge Hogan's decision was appealed to the Ninth Circuit Court of Appeals and was still pending at the time of this writing.

Approximately one month after the second Ninth Circuit Court decision, the United States Second Circuit Court of Appeals (which includes the states of New York, Connecticut and Vermont) ruled on April 2, 1996, that the two New York state statutes that ban assisted suicide violate the Fourteenth Amendment (Burns, 1996). In *Quill v. Vacco*, the Court stated that "the right to refuse medical treatment has long been recognized in New York" (1996: 726). The Court invoked the words of Judge Cardozo, who wrote in *Schloendorff v. Society of New York Hospital* in 1914 that under New York law, "every human being of adult years and sound mind has a right to determine what shall be done with his own body" (80 F.3d 716: 726).

Even though the Second Circuit reached the same conclusion as the Ninth Circuit, the Court used a different legal theory. In ruling that the state statutes banning assisted suicide violate the equal protection clause of the Fourteenth Amendment, the Court asserted that the laws unconstitutionally discriminate against persons who are terminally ill but are not on life support systems because they or their physicians cannot legally turn off the life sustaining mechanisms.

The Attorneys General of both Washington and New York have announced their intentions to appeal the Ninth Circuit and Second Circuit decisions to the United States Supreme Court (Burns, 1996). If the Supreme Court decides to hear the cases involving the two appellate rulings, the High Court's judgment is expected to generate as much, if not more controversy than the *Roe v. Wade* decision.

The next chapter primarily expands upon the Default Model, which serves as the conceptual framework for this study and explains why physician assisted suicide became a direct democracy issue. Additionally, some of the basic problems associated with physician assisted suicide are discussed.

NOTES

[1]See Humphry's book, *Let Me Die Before I Wake* (1981) for detailed accounts of assisted suicide.

[2]Interestingly, many European codes recognize the concept of "homicide upon request," which allows a judge to mitigate the sentence of an individual who has committed a homicide when that individual performs the homicide at the request of the deceased (Sayid, 1983: 553). The motive behind the crime is of substantial importance. Thus, while assisted suicide is not legal, the courts certainly treat these cases differently. In doing so, one might assert that the courts are tacitly attempting to recognize an individual's right of self-determination.

[3]While the whole issue of intent is both compelling and relevant, it is a consuming and lengthy topic which will not be addressed in depth in an effort not to diverge from the primary issue.

[4]See *Bartling v. Superior Court,* 163 Cal. App. 3d 186, 209 Cal. Rptr. 220 (Ct. Appl. 1984).

[5]Schaffer (1986) defines facilitating suicide as providing a suicidal individual with helpful but not necessary assistance. For example, a person facilitates another's suicide by addressing suicide notes. Aiding or assisting suicide is defined according to Schaffer as providing a suicidal individual with the means to commit suicide (e.g., providing a gun).

[6]*State v. Bouse*, 1953, is often cited for the difference between aiding a suicide and murdering a willing victim:

> The Oregon statute on assistance to suicide does not contemplate active participation by one in the overt act directly causing death. It contemplates some participation in the events leading up to the commission of the final overt act, such as furnishing the means of bringing about death - the fun, the knife, the poison, or providing the water, for the use of the person who himself commits the act of self-murder. But where a person actually performs, or actively assists in performing, the overt act resulting in death, such as shooting or stabbing the victim, administering the poison, or holding one under water until death takes place by drowning, his act

constitutes murder, and it is wholly immaterial whether this act is committed pursuant to an agreement with the victim, such as a mutual suicide pact.

[7]Readers should see Chapter Two for a complete discussion of advance directives.

[8]According to Dana Hirsch (1990), most jurisdictions in the United States permit voluntary passive euthanasia, which is commonly characterized as the right to withdraw or refuse medical treatment.

[9]Refer to Do-Not-Resuscitate legislation in Chapter Two for more details.

[10]Although *Roe v. Wade* balanced a mother's fundamental right to make personal decisions about private matters against a state's interest in forbidding abortions, the Court ultimately ruled that an individual does possess a fundamental right to self-determination (410 U.S. 113 (1973)). This protection is particularly important in areas of moral controversy such as abortion, contraception, and euthanasia, where the right to privacy acts to protect private decision making in personal matters (Wolhandler, 1984: 370).

[11]Because Karen did not have a flat electroencephalogram (EEG), exhibited involuntary muscle activity, responded to pain, light, sound and smell, she did not meet the Harvard Medical School criteria for brain death (Humphry & Wickett, 1990).

[12]According to Humphry, the doctrine of informed consent establishes a dual responsibility for physicians: (1) a duty to disclose to the patient the nature and ramifications of available treatments, and (2) a duty to obtain the patient's consent to any treatment prior to its administration. In addition, physicians must also inform the patient of treatment alternatives (1990: 195).

[13]The right of informed consent does not include the right to refuse nutrition/hydration. It refers strictly to medical procedures and treatments.

[14]See Norman Cantor, 1973; Martha Alys Matthews, 1987; George Smith, 1989; and Derek Humphry & Ann Wickett, 1990.

[15]While Quinlan and Cruzan were presumably not considered terminally ill, their cases differed from Bouvia's since they were both in the persistent vegetative state. Consequently, it can be argued that they did not particularly enjoy any quality of life, as opposed to Bouvia who was still mentally coherent and could still enjoy intellectual

stimulation (e.g., talking with friends and reading books). Most importantly, Bouvia's case could be classified as active euthanasia, while the cases of Quinlan and Cruzan fell under the passive euthanasia category.

[16]Pieter V. Admiraal (1986), noted Dutch euthanasia expert, asserts that euthanasia should be practiced only by the attending physician, and not by the nursing profession, relatives, or unqualified third parties.

[17]The preservation of life was a primary concern to Glendale Adventist Hospital, which submitted a declaration indicating that it is a Christian, pro-life oriented hospital. Disconnecting life-supporting mechanisms would be considered inconsistent with the primary task of healing.

[18]See *People v. Roberts*, 211 Mich. 187, 178 N.W. (1920).

[19]Judith Daar (1995: 827) suggests that the *Gilbert* case demonstrates that the "courts are simply unwilling...or unable to consider killing to end suffering as anything but murder."

[20]Dana Hirsch (1990) raises an interesting comparison between Switzerland and the United States. In the United States, a person's motive is not considered when guilt or length of sentencing is being determined. Conversely, however, in Switzerland, an individual's motive is considered relevant in these same circumstances. This differentiates the "cold blooded killer" who is motivated by sheer malice, for example, from the person who is merely attempting to relieve another's suffering. In addition, the person's motive bears on the quality of the person's character, which serves as an indicator as to whether or not the individual will commit the crime again (Sayid, 1983).

[21]In February 1993, Michigan Governor Engler signed a bill banning assisted suicides for terminally ill patients. The measure makes assisted suicide a felony punishable by up to four years in prison and a $2,000 fine (*Los Angeles Times*, December 4, 1992). Some opponents, however, consider it to be a hastily written law and on January 27, 1994, Oakland County Circuit Judge Jessica Cooper was the third judge to rule against the ban. Wayne County Circuit Judge, Richard C. Kaufman had already ruled on Monday, December 14, 1993 that there is a constitutional right of "rational" suicide, also

implying that the ban on assisted suicide is too broad (Pasternack & Shryer, 12/14/93: A26).

[22]In August 1996, Richard Thompson, the county prosecutor, who for years attempted to stop Dr. Kevorkian from assisting in suicides was defeated in a Republican primary election that was viewed as a referendum on the way he handled the issue of physician assisted suicide. Thompson had been criticized for prosecuting Dr. Kevorkian in what citizens considered to be two expensive and overly publicized trials (*New York Times*, 8/8/96: A23).

[23]Compassion in Dying consists of approximately twenty-five volunteers and 1,400 financial backers, counsels and supports individuals who seek help in ending their lives in the final stages of terminal illness (Balazar, 1994: A5). The group helps only those who are terminally ill and have been determined by their physician to have six months or less to live, and who have undergone a mental screening (Balazar, 1994: A5). If these criteria are fulfilled, it is the patient's responsibility to obtain enough barbiturates from his/her physician to enable the suicide to happen. Some patients request that Compassion in Dying volunteers be present when they are about to commit suicide, although the organization is vague about how many suicides its volunteers have witnessed (Balazar, 1994: A5).

[24]In *United States v. Salerno* 481 U.S. 745 (1987), the Supreme Court held that a statute should not be considered unconstitutional on its face unless challengers demonstrate that "no set of circumstances exists under which the law would be valid."

IV

Policy-making By Default: The Initiative

This chapter addresses why the initiative is frequently the vehicle of last resort in attempting to legalize an issue. Why and how do certain subjects gain public acceptance? I suggest that when the Default Model encounters the right timing coupled with a lengthy gestation period, the result can be quite satisfactory. One of the main objectives of this section is to explore the politics of physician assisted suicide within the context of this framework. The history and mechanics of the initiative process is also included for the purpose of understanding the present and long-term implications of direct democracy.

A discussion of how certain topics become objects of direct democracy must begin with the question of how policy is *usually* made. While many different scholars posit their own "formulas" for policy-making, there are certain elements which all of these formulas share. Policy-making involves the interaction between legislatures (federal or state) and the general populace. So called "linkage institutions," parties, elections, interest groups and the media function as the interactive forces between the people and policy-makers. This does not, however, guarantee that even though a concern has been voiced, in a public opinion poll for example, that the problem will be addressed by public officials. Therein lies the challenge inasmuch as articulating a perceived problem is rarely problematic. The difficulty lies in finding the means whereby it will be addressed.

Sometimes, the courts are called upon to "fix what's broken" in the same or similar way that the legislatures might be called upon. The fact that the courts are a passive institution, means that they must wait to be approached with an issue. Hoefler and Kamoie (1994) assert that [state] courts are in a "buck stops here" situation: they cannot go out of their way to make policy, but when something like the right-to-die falls into their lap, they are obliged to deal with it (p. 221). Having heard and decided such seminal cases as *Quinlan* (1976) and *Cruzan* (1990), state courts are given the credit for recognizing and asserting a terminally ill individual's right to refuse medical treatment (Hoefler and Kamoie, 1991). This implies that they sometimes serve as "alternative" policy-makers, promulgating public policy when legislatures choose not to place an issue on their agenda. Hoefler and Kamoie (1994) suggest that "legislatures also enjoy the luxury of benign neglect . . . That is, when clear policy solutions to problems do not present themselves together with political impetus for policy making, legislatures defer to the courts."

How is it that only certain issues garner the attention of policy-makers? Numerous elements are involved. Cobb and Elder (1983: 86) assert that three major components determine whether or not policy-makers will take notice of a subject:

1. How serious is the problem/issue?
2. Does the problem fall within the realm of government?
3. Is this issue important enough to a particular decision-maker so that he or she will champion its cause?

These elements point to what is recognized as a crucial part of policy-making: agenda setting. Whether or not a perceived problem is placed onto the political agenda[1] is largely dependent upon how the previous three questions are answered. According to Baumgartner & Jones (1993) a central concept to agenda setting is issue definition. Priority of an issue on the agenda may be variable depending upon its perceived seriousness. How serious is the problem and its consequences? Rochefort and Cobb (1994) use the word "severity" in determining whether an issue is important enough to make it onto a crowded agenda.

If the problems surrounding an issue are deemed "severe" enough, public assumption may be that once on the government agenda, passage is a virtual certainty. This is generally unrealistic and eventual passage of a proposed law or change in a law is contingent upon what Kingdon describes as an "open policy window." Specifically, policy windows present opportunities for action on the measure in concern.[2] Kingdon asserts that sometimes these windows open naturally (e.g., a policy comes up for renewal). At other times, windows open due to a change in the political stream, such as a change in administration or a shift in the national mood. For example, in the 1980s, many local communities and law enforcement officials were concerned about the growing use of cocaine, even though Congress was not giving it priority status. However, the death of basketball star Len Bias in June, 1986 from a cocaine overdose basically precipitated a "crisis" and attracted much public attention (Wise, 1991). Ultimately, this prompted Congress to enact the Anti-Drug Act by October of that same year (Wise, 1991). This is one instance where the policy-making and linkage institution(s) (i.e. the media), were effective in two ways: (1) in addressing and exposing an issue which the public recognized as a problem and (2) in prompting the formal policy-making institutions to respond to the issue.

In a similar way, there have been many occurrences which could have and should have created the impetus for placing assisted suicide onto the (federal) governmental agenda. Bosso (1994) suggests that when a highly charged issue is involved and there appears to be a lack of consensus in the nation, legislatures are loathe to proceed without overwhelming public support.

While the right-to-die and specifically physician assisted suicide is not a new topic, it was not until the late 1970s that the movement encouraging its legalization truly gained its momentum. The controversy over planned death for the terminally ill proved to be as heated and as passionate as the abortion debate. Albeit covertly, euthanasia had been in practice for many decades, and attempts were continually being made to increase and enhance public awareness. Then, almost all at once, a number of successive occurrences "awakened" the citizenry (but presumably not the policy-makers), bringing the realization that the subject could no longer be avoided, and thereby raising the "severity" index (Rochefort & Cobb, 1994). The following events can be credited with the raising of public consciousness regarding patient autonomy and the right-to-die.[3]

- In the 1970s, state legislatures began to enact living will laws, followed by laws in the 1980s advocating the use of the durable power of attorney.

- The media focused on two landmark cases, Quinlan in the 1970s and Cruzan in the 1980s, both of which raised questions regarding patient autonomy.

- The 1980s witnessed the publication of Derek Humphry's *Let Me Die Before I Wake* (1981) (first edition), a book which recounts many instances of active voluntary euthanasia in which individuals were forced to enlist the help of friends and/or relatives, and Betty Rollin's *Last Wish*, in which she describes how she helped her mother die.

- Derek Humphry's "how to commit suicide" book, *Final Exit* (1991), topped the *New York Times* bestseller list and was translated into several different languages.

- In 1990, the United States Congress enacted the Patient Self-Determination Act, which requires medical facilities to inform patients upon admission of their right to articulate their wishes in the form of an advance directive.

- Retired Pathologist Dr. Jack Kevorkian (nick-named "Dr. Death" by the media), aided his first suicide in 1990.

- Propositions 119 (1991) and 161 (1992), both advocating active voluntary euthanasia, made it onto the Washington and California state ballots respectively.

- A 1991 Gallup Poll indicated that 65% of the population supports physician aid-in-dying.

- Physician assisted suicide essentially became accepted in the Netherlands. Physicians are allowed to aid patients in dying without the fear of prosecution as long as they adhere to certain criteria.

- The AIDS epidemic and the increase in cancer rates in the 1990s combined forces with the events just described to create a heightened awareness with respect to end-of-life issues.

In spite of these pivotal events, the issue never made it onto the national government agenda. According to Humphry and Wickett (1991) policy-makers in a few states sponsored physician assisted suicide bills.[4] The attempts, however, were sporadic. The first bill championing physician assisted suicide was in Nebraska in 1937 and was sponsored by Dr. Inez Philbrick, a former member of the

University of Nebraska faculty (p. 14). The bill, entitled the Voluntary Euthanasia Act, was referred to committee and ultimately died there.

Again in 1939, a bill to legalize euthanasia in New York was proposed in response to inquiries to the Euthanasia Society of America from persons suffering from incurable diseases (p. 15). It primarily concentrated on terminally ill adults and was never introduced into the legislature.

Humphry & Wickett (1991) outline the early legislative activity and suggest that it was fueled by the growing number of court cases in England and America since 1920 that revolved around mercy killings, assisted suicide, and suicide due to terminal illness. Because no two results were the same, the ultimate goal of the proposed legislation was consistency.

According to Humphry and Wickett, another attempt was made. In 1941, the Euthanasia Society of America sent a questionnaire to more than twenty thousand physicians. Remarkably, four out of five doctors responded that they were in favor of legalizing euthanasia for persons with incurable diseases. Because the results were so encouraging, the Society decided to introduce a "mercy death" bill into the New York State legislature, but due to the lack of a sponsor, the bill failed. Even more important is the fact that in spite of this, a campaign was launched, and a petition was circulated to demonstrate support. Once again, the Euthanasia Society was unable to find a sponsor. Public consciousness, however, had been raised as a result of this effort.

The Euthanasia Society did make a final attempt in 1952 to secure legislative backing for its bill by submitting to the Senate President a petition measuring nine feet, signed by two thousand voters. Arthur Wickes, who was the Senate President at that time, refused to act on behalf of the petition, and the bill was never introduced into the legislature (Humphry and Wickett, 1991).

There have also been some attempts in the past twenty-five years at introducing physician assisted suicide legislation. In 1991, Oregon's senior senator, Frank Roberts, and The Hemlock Society jointly sponsored the Death With Dignity Act (Humphry, 1993: 62). It went before the Oregon legislature, but never made it out of committee (Humphry, 1993: 62). Opposition was encountered on two fronts. Legislators appeared to be ignorant of the subject, which indicated that they did not care to research it and churches (with the exception of the

Unitarians) were vehemently opposed to the issue (Humphry, 1993: 62).

In early 1992, legislators in Maine, New Hampshire, Iowa, and Michigan introduced into their assemblies laws which if passed, would legalize aid-in-dying. While the laws were well-intentioned, Humphry asserts that these laws were not well drafted, largely because the draftspersons had little experience with the subject (1993: 61). The New Hampshire bill was the only one which sought to allow a physician to provide a lethal prescription for a terminally ill individual (Humphry, 1993: 61). The other bills were broader and included provisions for death by prescription overdose as well as lethal injection administered by a physician. In spite of this, the New Hampshire bill died an early death, but there is occasional talk of it being revived.[5]

Why were (are) policy-makers essentially hesitant to champion the physician assisted suicide cause? Three reasons seem plausible: (1) an assisted suicide "crisis" did not seem to be at the helm; (2) the timing was not "right"; and (3) the topic had not undergone a sufficient gestation period. The next section examines these claims.

TIMING: WHEN AN IDEA'S TIME HAS COME

Implicit in the concept of an open policy window, as Kingdon (1984) also asserts, is the notion that a particular idea's time "has come." In this way, decision-makers and the general citizenry become willing and able to address a concern, whether it be a change in an already existing policy or the implementation of a new one. In this instance, public opinion polls and the national mood indicate that not only is it time for a change, but that the public is *ready* for such a change. An open policy window is indeed a fortuitous occurrence. But it takes a tremendous amount of patience and maneuvering to secure passage of a bill. For those groups and individuals who possess a pressing desire to have their issue addressed, the wait may be a long one, depending upon the strength of their contacts with government officials and the financial status of the organization. The reality is that it is a virtual impossibility to attract attention to an issue without an "inside" person to further the cause, especially if the time is not "right."

The literature suggests that the notion of an idea whose time has come is somewhat ambiguous. In describing the diffusion[6] of no-fault divorce, Herbert Jacob argues that "in the absence of another compelling explanation, it is perhaps plausible to argue that it became nearly universal simply because the time was ripe for such a measure" (1988: 92). He acknowledges that there is no fool-proof way of discerning when the "time is ripe," and that it may be reasonable to maintain that policies win acceptance *simply because* the time is ripe (Jacob, 1988: 93). The compelling question is, when is the time *not* ripe? One might assert that this, too, is an ambiguous question since each particular subject invites its own set of circumstances. In the case of no-fault divorce, the social environment provided fertile ground for its spread. "Social Environment" at the time of no-fault divorce law encompassed the feminist movement, no-fault being adopted in the field of automobile insurance, and the declining social stigma for divorcees coupled with the growing opinion that divorce was often the best solution to an unsatisfactory marriage (Jacob, 1988). While these phenomena culminated to provide the impetus for such changes, Jacob asserts that the circular nature of the argument renders the "time is ripe" explanation unacceptable as the *complete* reason for its passage. Specifically, the acceptance or rejection of a policy becomes the indicator of the ripeness of the times, which is then used to explain the fate of the policy proposal. Thus, it becomes difficult to determine the cause and effect.

Nevertheless, no-fault divorce was at first perceived as a "politically delicate" topic and leaders were not particularly enthusiastic to voice an opinion on the subject, let alone trumpet its cause. In most cases, leaders such as Governor Rockefeller in New York and Governor Reagan in California demonstrated a "benign neutrality" toward the issue meaning that they were not involved in the early stages of formulating the bill (Jacob, 1988: 89). Ultimately, the governor had to sign the bill or at least not veto it (Jacob, 1988: 89). In the case of New York, leaders became involved with the issue only after a political entrepreneur pushed it onto the legislative agenda with vigorous advocacy and coalition building (Jacob, 1988: 90). In the end, however, it was the legislatures which can be credited with bringing about the desired end result.

Contrary to the no-fault divorce example for which the formal policy-making institutions actually worked, some scholars remain doubtful of Congress' ability to legislate effectively.[7] Divided government, the system of checks and balances, separation of powers, and the decentralized nature of government as a whole, (including Congressional committees), paralyzes Congress and inhibits it from producing comprehensive, coherent policies (Wise, 1991). Once thought to be safeguards against the tyranny of the majority, the system of checks and balances and the separation of powers often results in deadlock or decision-making compromised to such an extent that the original purpose is greatly diluted. Party government, created to ensure diverse and innovative policy-making, now lends itself to biased policy-making (Cox & Kernell, 1991). The initiative process, however, represents pluralistic policy-making and a more direct way of attempting to achieve passage of a measure.

The Equal Rights Amendment (ERA), is a useful example of Congress' attempt to legislate effectively and also of the time not being right in spite of the appropriate social environment of the 1970s. In March 1972, the Amendment passed in the United States Senate with a vote of eighty-four to eight. It was relatively well-received by policy-makers and citizens and between 1972 to 1982, a majority of Americans consistently told interviewers that they favored amending the Constitution, so that it would include equal rights for women (Mansbridge, 1986). On June 30, 1982, however, the deadline for signing the amendment passed with only thirty-five of the required thirty-eight states having ratified (Mansbridge, 1986: 1). Why, when after the feminist movement of the late 1960s and 1970s, when the public was presumably ready for such a change, did this amendment fail? Mansbridge argues that in spite of the public's seeming "readiness" for such a modification, the American public simply did not want any significant change in gender roles, whether at work, at home, or in society at large (1986: 1).

Although the timing then, and in retrospect, seemed to have been perfect, a major alteration, such as equal rights for women as mandated by law was perhaps too new and perceived as having too much of a significant impact in too many areas, especially to legislators in wavering states (Mansbridge, 1986). Thus, the issue may have lacked a sufficient period of gestation and consequently, when it came time to offer support for passage, legislators and the public may have felt the ERA was lacking in familiarity. Additionally, this was a politically "delicate" subject which would entail polarizing a certain, and perhaps substantial, portion of a politician's constituency should he/she take a stand. Furthermore, much of the support for the Amendment was superficial, because it was based on support for abstract rights, not for real changes (Mansbridge, 1986: 2).

Here again lies the dilemma: there is no fool-proof way of gauging the right time and what constitutes a sufficient gestation period. Even though ERA efforts were a significant part of the feminist era, and women were making great strides in furthering their own autonomy, bad timing, coupled with the lack of "insider" support and perhaps the absence of substantive information regarding future effects, ensured the ultimate demise of the ERA. Thus, while timing cannot be considered the only factor in the defeat of the ERA, it can certainly be identified as a major one. Further inquiry would render interesting results, one way or another, as to whether at present, the timing is right for re-introduction and passage of an equal rights amendment.

The direct democracy history of physician assisted suicide underscores the notion of timing. Clearly, in 1991 and 1992, voters were not ready to take the large step of affirming the right of a terminally ill individual to request aid-in-dying. Arguably, the issue may have been too new and revolutionary at that time. In 1994, however, Oregon voters were ready to pass Measure 16 which did not contain the loopholes and other problems that plagued Propositions 119 and 161. In addition to the fact that Measure 16 was stronger in terms of safeguards for the patient and physician, its passage signified that the timing was finally right. The electorate had become had had ample time to become familiar with the issue. In this way, Propositions 119 and 161 can be considered learning experiences, since the lessons garnered from their respective failures were what facilitated the creation and eventual passage of Measure 16.

In part, the success of Measure 16 can be attributed to issue redefinition (Baumgartner and Jones, 1994). The "losers" redefine the points of controversy to their advantage, and in the process, may garner support from previous opposers or uninvolved citizens (Baumgartner & Jones, 1994: 11). As such, the image of physician assisted suicide was reinvented. The final version of Measure 16 contained much stronger safeguards such as:

- A fifteen day waiting period from the time of the initial oral request.
- A fifteen day waiting period from the time of the initial oral request and a forty-eight hour waiting period from the time of written request.
- The written request must be witnessed by two persons (one person must be unrelated to the patient)
- Excludes non-residents and physicians who were not licensed to practice in Oregon.
- Unlike Propositions 119 and 161, Measure 16 differs significantly in that it prohibits the physician from administering the drug overdose. The exclusive role of the physician is to prescribe the drugs.

Thus, in addressing the major point of contention, namely lack of safeguards, which contributed to the failure of both Propositions 119 and 161, Measure 16 came to be regarded as more controlled and safer way of allowing terminally ill patients to request aid-in-dying.

When a proposed change of law or implementation of policy fails within the formal policy-making institutions, the initiative is often utilized as a response to the lack of continual attention by policy-makers. The following section explores the origins of the initiative and discusses some of the perceived pros and cons of its use.

THE INITIATIVE: PURPOSE AND PRACTICE

The initiative was born out of the Progressive Movement of the early 1900s and echoed the thoughts of Thomas Jefferson, who believed that the will of the people was the only legitimate foundation of any government; and that "even a deficient popular government" was preferable to the most "glorious autocratic one" (Cronin, 1989: 40). Specifically, the initiative was introduced in 1911 and was intended to check the influence of business monopolies that dominated the legislature (Barnes, 1990: 2047). Two general beliefs predominated during this period:

1. political organizations were corrupt and many of the ills of American democracy were directly attributable to political

parties, party officials, state legislatures, mayors, and city governments; and

2. individual citizens desired to exercise greater control over government and were capable of determining the public good for themselves. Promoted by reformist progressives, the initiative was seen as a way to circumvent a legislature that was corrupt and controlled by special interests or party bosses (Barnes, 1991).

During the early decades of the 1900s, the initiative was used frequently, but in the early 1940s and the years thereafter, there was a definite decline in use. In the 1970s and 1980s, however, there was substantially greater use of the initiative and this increased activity seems to have peaked in the 1990s.[8]

The passage of Proposition 13 in 1978 can and should be considered the catalyst for renewed faith in the initiative. Proposition 13 focused nationwide attention on the public's right and desire to participate in controversial tax decision making, as Californians voted to cut their property taxes by at least half (Cronin, 1989: 3) and the eventual passage of the Initiative greatly altered the political landscape of not only California, but of many states. It had two major effects: it triggered similar tax-slashing measures, both as bills and as direct legislation by the people in numerous other states (twenty-seven tax or spending limit movements in nineteen states) (Cronin, 1989), and it encouraged conservative interest groups to use the initiative process to achieve some of their goals. In addition, those states which did not possess the initiative and referendum became inspired, so to speak, by the citizen participation garnered by Proposition 13. Consequently, governors and legislative leaders (primarily Republican) in several states, such as Alabama, Georgia, Hawaii, Minnesota, New Jersey, New York, Rhode Island, and Texas, led efforts to get the initiative and referendum legislatively authorized in their jurisdictions. In fact, some scholars assert that public policy agenda in some states (i.e. California) has shifted from the legislature to the initiative process (Barnes, 1990: 2047).[9]

Inherent in the notion of citizen law-makers is the central question of competency. How competent and informed are those who vote on the ballot issues? According to Cronin, voters are not as competent as one would wish, yet not as ill informed or irrational as critics often insist (1989: 87). Who is it that participates in issue voting? Generally, the "typical" initiative voter possesses all or some of the following characteristics: civic mindedness, financial stability, and higher education.[10] Most importantly, however, people are more likely to vote when an issue captures their attention (i.e. the death penalty, gay rights, AIDS, gun control) (Cronin, 1989; Magleby, 1984). In truth, "politically delicate" issues, frequently avoided by policy-makers, function as election day catalysts for initiative voters.[11] The fact that it is frequently these politically delicate issues which make it onto the ballots is perhaps accountable for stimulating voter turnout.

In spite of the many virtues of the initiative, certain aspects of the process prove troubling to some scholars and lawmakers and it is presumably these objections which impede adoption of the initiative in other states:

- Policy-makers and scholars alike object to the fact sometimes an ill-considered measure wins approval simply because an uniformed electorate actually went to the polls and won the necessary majority. It is, however, important to realize that occasional bad decision-making is also sometimes a product of the formal policy-making institutions. For example, the U.S. Supreme Court decisions, *Plessy v. Ferguson* (1896) and *Korematsu v. United States* (1944) are no longer considered constitutionally sound decisions and are based on unacceptable arguments (Cronin, 1989). Likewise, former President Franklin Roosevelt's attempt to pack the Supreme Court is not remembered as one of his most sensible decisions. Hence, bad policy-making is not exclusive to the initiative process or the average voter.

- Some scholars maintain that initiatives are a tool of special interests (Schmidt, 1989). This may be so, but is it necessarily a negative point? The main purpose of the initiative is to offer politically motivated individuals a way of taking action on issues which they feel are important. Just because special interests avail themselves of the initiative does not mean that they have a monopoly on the policy-making process, especially since each measure must be submitted for public approval and is (sometimes) later subject to judicial examination.

- In addition, opponents argue that initiatives enhance minority rule because many voters do not vote on them. Studies comparing participation of initiatives with participation in state legislative races have found initiative turnout to be just as high or higher (Schmidt, 1989: 38). At some point, what needs to be recognized is that since initiatives are subject oriented, some propositions will invite more or less activism, depending upon how passionately the public feels about the particular issue. In addition, initiative turnout may be quite dependent on the number of propositions that are on the ballot. A ballot full of initiatives may intimidate members of the voting population and deter them from voting. As is the case in California, a state known for inundating its ballot with propositions, the amount of information which is sent to voters is often so vast and detailed that voters do not take the time to read all of the literature. To presume that they will or should take the time to thoroughly read the information is somewhat unreasonable, because the materials are often dense and lengthy, and everyone cannot be expected to be interested in each proposition.
- Initiatives create a tyranny of the majority in that individuals and groups are subject to the policy prerogatives of those groups who are able to get their measures on the ballot. What is often overlooked is that, as mentioned earlier, initiatives are subject to judicial review and thus must conform to the federal constitution, which protects against such a violation. In fact, an inherent objective of the initiative process is to guard *against* tyranny of the majority by granting the smaller, less visible groups access to the political system.
- The people cannot be trusted to vote intelligently on complex issues. This contradicts the findings of a 1984 Gallup Poll, which concluded that "the judgment of the American people is extraordinarily sound. The public is always ahead of its leaders." (Schmidt, 1989: 40). Furthermore, asserting that citizens lack the capability to vote intelligently contradicts the basic intent of democratic theory: self-governance.

With respect to physician assisted suicide, the initiative can be considered a tool which is being utilized by a special interest. In actuality, were it not for direct democracy, the issue might still be on the periphery and public awareness might still be lacking. The Default Model explains why legalization of controversial topics sometimes has to be sought through direct democracy efforts.

THE DEFAULT MODEL

When the legislatures choose not to address certain issues and the courts have either failed to be decisive or have not had the opportunity to address those issues, the initiative process becomes the vehicle by which citizens seek take action and influence public policy. In effect, the initiative process is sometimes employed to bypass the legislative process when issues of specific concern have not been placed on the main agenda. Consequently, it is sometimes by default that individuals must turn to the initiative process as a means of creating and enacting new laws. While this is not an entirely new concept, the literature on direct democracy seems to be lacking in explanation as to exactly why and how certain issues eventually become objects of direct democracy. The focus in the literature has primarily been on the pros and cons of the initiative process and its history and relatively little attention has been paid to documenting the last resort phenomenon. The Default Model contributes in this manner.

Hence, the conceptual framework for this study is centered around the Default Model, which seeks to explain how issue salience and other policy-making indicators can function as initiative process catalysts. The foundation for the Default model is based on three assumptions:

1. The formal political institutions, such as the courts and legislatures have in some way failed in promulgating some type of coherent policy regarding a particular issue such as physician assisted suicide;
2. A certain segment of the public (which has mobilized into interest groups in an effort to collectively attract attention to a given topic) is "restless" for some action on a particular issue (e.g., physician assisted suicide); and

3. Topics such as assisted suicide have become ballot issues for the same reason that the courts and legislatures have been unable to affirm their constitutionality; namely the inherent moral and ethical composition of the subject.

It merits repeating that the Default Model suggests that the initiative is not so much a "tool" as it is a last resort (see Figure 4-1). Basically, when a subject is perceived by the legislatures as too controversial, "politically delicate," or "too hot to handle," policy-makers back away from it (Kingdon, 1984) and initiative efforts can be anticipated.

What makes a topic "too hot to handle?" With respect to physician assisted suicide, Tatalovich and Danes (1988) offer accurate insight. As discussed in Chapter Two, the subject is clearly one involving social regulation. According to Tatalovich and Danes, *what* is being regulated is not an economic transition but a social relationship, defined by community values, moral codes, and norms of personal conduct (Tatalovich and Danes, 1988: 2). They further assert that this type of social regulation provokes intense, persistent controversy. As a result, policy-makers are loath to create too much debate by taking a stand one way or the other. After all, doing so would almost certainly alienate that segment of his/her constituency which did not agree with the official's position.

In asserting that matters involving social regulatory policy are not a high legislative priority due to their innately volatile nature, one might expect that the courts would take over. In some areas involving social regulatory policy, this has indeed occurred. The courts did grapple with the sticky abortion issue in the 1973 landmark case, *Roe v. Wade* and some scholars assert that the right-to-die issue is similar to abortion since it concerns the preservation of life, albeit at opposite ends of the life cycle (Glick & Hays, 1991). Abortion is one example where politicians continue to actively voice their opinion, and in doing so, choose to accept the label "pro-life" or "pro-choice." Similar to the right-to-die issue, the debate involves polarization of both sides. There is no "middle" view and consequently, politicians are frequently judged based on their view of abortion. In truth, the pro or con stance can either increase or decrease number of votes in his/her favor.

Contrary to popular belief, the abortion issue had been around long before it surfaced on the national agenda in 1973. It was first

Figure 4.1: The Default Model

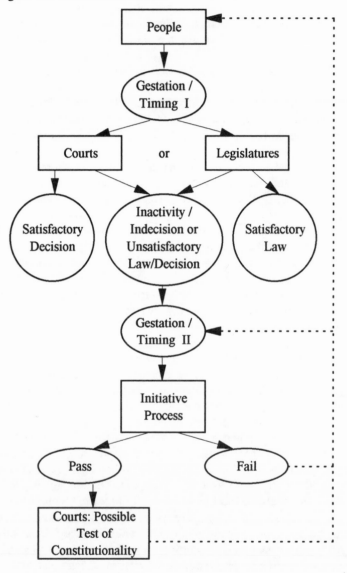

regulated in 1821 when Connecticut enacted the first statute outlawing abortion after quickening (when there is undeniable movement of the fetus) (Tatalovich, 1988). Ensuing years of information and increasing awareness culminated into much political activity.[12] It bears questioning whether in 1973 abortion was an idea whose time who had come or if a liberal U.S. Supreme Court forced it on the public. Then again, one might reason that after having been exposed since 1821, the "free-wheeling" '60s and 1970s were fertile ground for such a big change--the "social environment" was right. One might also conjecture that similar to V.O. Key's theory of political realignment, in which approximately every 36 years the electorate redefines its party loyalty--an activity which is precipitated by some other major occurrence (i.e. the Great Depression) making it a prime time for such re-identification--social change requires a similar time table. A number of years pass with relative stability--things remain the same--and then a plethora of activity abounds. The momentum created by public opinion, debate and a broader mind-set (perhaps stimulated by a major event, such as a war (i.e. Vietnam in the 1960s)) allows these changes to happen. As such, a gestation period in which the public becomes familiarized with and decisive about a given issue (i.e. abortion) eventually contributes to the right timing.

So then even if the general public has resorted to using the initiative process to encourage passage of a physician assisted suicide measure, the timing must be right in order for it to pass. Again the issue arises: when is the time "right?" Kingdon (1984) argues that even policy-makers are not sure how or even why a subject gets "hot." He acknowledges that the process is an untidy one and confusing at best, largely because it is so difficult to predict when the time *is* right or when it *will be* right.

When the Default Model encounters the right "timing," coupled with a sufficient period of gestation, the result, as in the case of Measure 16, can be quite satisfactory to those citizens seeking legalization. This was also the case with respect for the quest for term limits. Term limits for members of Congress had been discussed for years, but proposals drew little support especially since it not only involved the tenure of their colleagues, but also their own. Not only were state legislators resistant, but the public was also growing increasingly frustrated with their unwillingness to squarely address the issue. The initiative process proved to be the answer and in 1990,

Colorado was the first state to vote on and approve such a measure (Jost, 1992).

The idea was not a new one. In fact, "rotation in office" was a popular concept in the 1700s and was even included in the Articles of Confederation. Indeed, it was customary in the 1800s for a House member to serve only one or two terms (Jost, 1992). Again, in the 1950s and into the 1980s, interest in limiting congressional tenure was apparent, but nothing was done. Then, in the 1990s, after the public had finally become aware of its merits, support was garnered and most of the propositions passed. In 1992, fourteen states enacted a term limits measure. In California, Proposition 140 was the term limits measure which passed, much to the chagrin of individuals such as former Assembly Speaker, Willie Brown.

The case of term limits fits nicely into the first two general stipulations of the Default Model. The legislatures rejected specific limits on congressional tenure. Consequently, a certain segment of the public became restless for some type of action and therefore undertook the effort to mobilize into groups so that money could be raised and support could be garnered. The fact of the matter is that there was little other choice. Since the legislatures were unwilling to face limiting their own terms and those of their political counterparts, the public had no other recourse. The initiative process provided a way of *doing* something, rather than just *talking* about their growing dissatisfaction with policy-makers. It offered citizens a means of expressing the public mood, which in this case, may simply have gone purposely unnoticed since term limits adversely affected the interests of the policy-makers.

Clearly, term limits was an idea whose time had come. The seed had germinated for years and it finally sprouted in the 1990s. The fact that it took so long for term limits to come to fruition can be considered both good and bad. On the positive side, when the initiatives finally did pass, they did so overwhelmingly.[13] Voters were clearly ready for the change. The negative aspect of how long it took for term limits to finally become a reality portends a pessimistic prediction for other "novel" ideas. Presumably, new ideas simply require a time lapse or period of gestation so that the citizenry can become acquainted with and accustomed to its implications. Hence, for an idea's time to come, it just takes time.

Allowing an idea to be fertilized in the minds of the public is not, however, a foolproof guarantee that a certain measure will pass. When Proposition 140 was placed on the California ballot in 1990, it was accompanied by another measure, Proposition 131. While Prop. 140 won approval with 52 percent of the vote, Proposition 131 was defeated (Alexander and Bhojwani, 1991). Both measures shared the common objective of limiting the terms of legislators' tenures. Other than that, the two were different in that Proposition 140 called for a six-year limit on tenure and Proposition 131 stipulated a 12 year limit. In truth, Proposition 140 was a much more stringent measure in that it called for a 40 percent reduction in the legislature's operating budget and the elimination of the legislative retirement system. Proposition 131, on the other hand, included public financing of campaigns, contribution limits and ethics provisions.

PHYSICIAN ASSISTED SUICIDE: THE DEFAULT MODEL APPLIED

While the Default Model is applicable to many issues, it bears special relevance to physician assisted suicide. As was discussed earlier in this chapter, certain events of the past twenty years inspired voter awareness and finally culminated in the early 1990s, engaging the public in heated debate about whether or not determining the time of one's own death is a basic civil liberty. It bears repeating that attempts had indeed been made in attempting to attract the attention of state legislatures, but to no avail. Logically, there was and still is not any reason to assume that policy-makers will address assisted suicide in a rational, objective manner, for two reasons. First, the issue is currently very "hot," and policy-makers are loathe to polarize their perspective constituencies by assuming any one position. Second, in spite of the AIDS epidemic, policy-makers do not perceive that any real crisis has occurred, forcing them to take action.

However, even though the AIDS epidemic has reached huge proportions, the idea of what type of death finally ensues (dignified and humane versus undignified and painful) has yet to become a central topic within the AIDS circle. As yet, however, there has only been somewhat limited activity from the AIDS activists. Some speculate that the AIDS community and the right-to-die faction keep each other at arms length in an effort to avoid the stigma of the other group (Friess, 1996). In addition, AIDS activists feel they have enough to do in getting the public to understand about AIDS (Friess, 1996). Another reason that individuals afflicted with AIDS avoid becoming active in the right-to-die movement is that the AIDS community places much emphasis on living with disease, rather than preparing for death (Friess, 1996). Nevertheless, people afflicted with the AIDS virus tend to be younger patients, more insistent on their civil rights than elderly patients with Alzheimer's disease or cancer (Friess, 1996) and as such, they are generally supportive, but have refrained from intense activism or verbal expression in favor of assisted suicide. But some support has been witnessed. For example, one of the patients in the *Compassion in Dying* case was a forty-four year old artist in the terminal phase of AIDS, who was concerned with end-of-life options. He died prior to the Court's ruling.

The history of assisted suicide made it almost inevitable that by "default," it would become an object of direct democracy. If the formal political institutions, such as the courts and legislatures failed in securing assisted suicide as an individual civil liberty, it is not only right, but absolutely necessary that the issue not be forgotten. The initiative process guarantees the latter and offers the opportunity for legalization even though there has been no real disaster which has precipitated an active euthanasia "crisis."[14] It was the efforts of individuals, whose "restlessness" provided the necessary impetus for getting the initiatives on the ballot. Chapter Five provides a thorough discussion of which interest groups and organizations participated and why. No matter how assisted suicide becomes legalized, the third component of the Default Model will remain constant: the inherent moral and ethical composition of the subject will continue to be troubling, thus inhibiting policy-makers from comprehensively addressing it.

The Default Model does not imply two extremes, the first being that legislatures always avoid "hot" topics and the second that the initiative process is always successful in bringing about decisiveness on these politically delicate subjects. In truth, there have also been plenty of instances in which the formal institutions actually worked, as was the case with no-fault divorce and with advance directives. In the case of living will laws, the state legislatures did act decisively and responsibly in responding to patient rights.[15] Legislation now permits individuals various degrees of advance control over medical treatment (Glick, 1990: 75) and amidst the controversies which surround the right-to-die, diffusion of innovations can be credited with how and why many states pursued adoption of advance directive laws (Glick, 1990).

In a similar way, the increase in judicial policy-making activity beginning in 1983 and continuing in 1984, and again in the late 1980s, undoubtedly is linked to the accumulation of information, news and political events surrounding the right-to-die which had been on state political agendas since the late 1960s (Glick, 1990: 78).[16] In fact, in 1983, a presidential commission was organized to consider various biomedical issues and public policy (*Deciding to Forego Life-sustaining Treatment*, 1983). The commission was not originally supposed to consider the right-to-die, but did so because members believed that it needed to be analyzed along with other policies (Glick, 1990).

Of particular importance with regard to the notion of gestation is that the right-to-die issue had been on the political agenda since the late 1960s and as discussed in Chapter Two, it was not until 1976 that California adopted the nation's first living will law (Glick, 1990). This fact supports the assertion that issue salience directly correlates with the amount of time a certain topic has been under public discussion. Issue awareness and familiarity is fostered by a lapse of time, although there is not any specific (uniform) amount of time which has been identified. In this way, in 1968, the Florida state legislature was the first (even before California) to consider the right-to-die, even though it did not result in any type of decisive policy, again demonstrating that gestation time is absolutely essential.

The advance directive example points to the possibility that physician assisted suicide may follow a similar path. One might argue that given time or an even longer gestation period, coupled with the accumulation of information, news and political events, the politicians and the public might be more apt to address patient rights in further depth and perhaps be more favorably inclined. Thus, as was the case with advance directives, a diffusion of innovation (Glick, 1991) regarding physician assisted suicide, wherein states choose to alter or "reinvent" the content of another state's law, might take place.[17]

To some degree this has already happened if one considers the fact that California modeled its 1992 Proposition 161 after

Washington state's 1991 Proposition 119.[18] Similarly, Oregon's Measure 16 was the ultimate outcome of both failed propositions. Individuals and groups in other states who are restless for legalization of physician assisted suicide may take their cue from Oregon and attempt to draft ballot initiatives which would achieve this result. In those states which do not have the direct democracy option, a lengthier gestation period and greater familiarity with the issue may encourage policy makers to become more inclined to seek introduction and passage of a physician assisted suicide bill if enough states have legalized it through the initiative process.

Even though time and the accumulation of information eventually prompted action on the part of the legislatures and courts for other issues, the process of legalization for physician assisted suicide will take much longer due to the sensitive nature of the subject. Certain current circumstances, however, may somewhat expedite activity. Since the AIDS epidemic has already created an impetus for those who are suffering from the disease and fear a long and humiliating death, it is perhaps reasonable to anticipate AIDS activists pushing for initiatives in other states which would allow AIDS patients to legally request aid in hastening their own deaths or the death of a friend or loved one (Gross, 1993). In a similar way, increasing cancer rates drive home the reality that the many years may be too long to wait for the legislature to legalize physician assisted suicide. Given the fact that these life threatening diseases are plaguing the population rendering no one immune to the possibility of having to suffer such a fate, patient autonomy seems of utmost importance.

Now that an understanding has been gleaned as to why physician assisted suicide became a ballot measure, the question remains as to what went on during the campaign(s). Exploring which components of Proposition 161 soured voters provides a foundation for examining election activities. Do the recent failures of physician assisted suicide measures reflect problems inherent within the process or mainly the subject itself? I maintain that the eventual defeat of Proposition 161 was due in large part to the lack of clarity regarding certain concepts and definitions related to Proposition 161 coupled with bad timing and an insufficient gestation period, rather than the fact that it was a direct democracy effort. Was there much support by interest groups? How, in particular, did senior interest groups react and/or act toward Proposition 161? Equally important, how did senior citizens feel about this measure? The next chapter addresses these questions and offers insight regarding the defeat of Proposition 161, the California Death With Dignity Act.

NOTES

[1] According to John Kingdon (1984), an agenda is defined as the list of subjects or problems to which government officials, and people outside of government closely associated with those officials, are paying some serious attention at any given time. Henceforth, Kingdon's definition will apply.

[2] Cobb and Elder (1983: 84-85) use the term "trigger device" to describe unforeseen events that help shape and activate issues.

[3] As will be discussed, the events and circumstances described above can be considered gestation activities, wherein the public becomes familiarized with, and decisive about, a given issue over an (extended) period of time.

[4] As of October, 1994, fourteen states had assisted suicide legislation pending. In seven states, the pending bills were in favor of legalizing assisted suicide. Regardless of the pro or con content, the assisted suicide bills are expected to die in or before they ever reach committee. In Rhode Island, for example, Catholic and anti-abortion groups launched a campaign to stop an assisted suicide bill from ever reaching the floor for debate (*Providence Journal-Bulletin*, 5/8/95: C1). Additionally, toward the end of 1996, a physician assisted suicide bill is expected to be introduced into the Massachusetts legislature.

[5] Because New Hampshire is one of the states which does not enjoy the privilege of the initiative, there is no option of expediting passage of such a law by taking it straight to the people for a vote.

[6] The process by which innovation (an idea perceived as new by an individual) spreads is called diffusion; it consists of the communication of a new idea in a social system over time (Walker, 1969; Gray, 1973).

[7] Even though the case of no-fault divorce involved activity on the part of the state legislatures, it still provides an effective commentary on the U.S. Congress since many of the same issues apply (e.g., checks and balances, separation of powers, etc.)

[8] Currently, only twenty-three states enjoy the privilege of the initiative.

[9] Interestingly, it has been suggested that the most important branch of government in California may be neither the legislative nor the executive, but the "initiative branch" (Barnes, 1990: 2047).

[10]Cronin cites opportunity costs (the time spent learning about the issue and ultimately voting on it) and information costs (the cost of gathering information about various aspects and the long-term implications of the issue) as more easily absorbed and justified by those who are civic minded, financially sound, and educated.

[11]"Politically delicate" issues are those of moral and ethical composition, which typically polarize a politician's constituency if he/she chooses to offer public support or opposition.

[12]Physician assisted suicide and abortion share the extreme opposition of the Catholic church. The prochoice coalition for both issues is composed of some single issue groups (i.e. The Hemlock Society and the National Abortion Rights Action League (NARAL)), but it is also composed of broad based interest groups, such as religious denominations (the Unitarian Church and the Protestant churches), health care organizations and groups in general whose agenda is basically a liberal one (i.e. the American Civil Liberties Union).

[13]In November, 1992, in four states, 74% or more of the voters supported congressional term limits; in all but three states, the measures passed with at least 60% (Jost, 1992)

[14]Derek Humphry maintains that "the likelihood of any legislature passing a bill for physician aid-in-dying is remote. Politicians are fearful of speaking out on ethical issues because the religious right would inevitably call for their defeat when they came up for re-election." (1993, p.62)

[15]The reader should recall that Chapter Two provides an overview of advance directives and other end-of-life documents.

[16]See Chapter Three for a history of court activity.

[17]Diffusion of innovation (Glick, 1991) will be discussed again in Chapter Six.

[18]Innovation through diffusion is not really applied to the literature on initiatives. I take this scholarly liberty in an effort to demonstrate a correlation between the three propositions.

V

Individual vs. Interest Group Behavior[1]

A number of scholars have suggested that euthanasia, the right-to-die, suicide, and related topics-such as physician assisted death-are particularly germane for older persons (for a review of several sources, see Post, 1993.). For example, Nuland (1994) asserts that some circumstances justify exceptions to the wrongfulness of taking one's own life, such as the unendurable infirmities and final devastations of crippling old age. Carpenter (1993) argues that the elderly have a unique claim to an ethical, unobstructed suicide that is based on the "developmental autonomy" that stems from their experience and wisdom. Leinbach (1993) suggests that these several topics have special meaning for many older Americans, while Glick asserts that "the elderly are disproportionately affected" by right-to-die issues, presumably because one is more susceptible to terminal illness in the later stages of life, making it necessary to address end-of-life concerns (1991:304).

This chapter explores the attitudes and activism of the elderly in relation to physician assisted death. It examines both the macro (aging interest group) and micro (individual) levels, using California's Proposition 161 as a case study. To determine old-age interest group attitudes and activism, I examined their advocacy levels on the ballot measure. To gauge attitudes at the micro level, a survey was conducted at an urban senior center in the Los Angeles area, exactly one week prior to the 1992 election. While based on a nonrepresentative sample of older people, this survey provides some interesting findings on older people's attitudes. It also can serve as the foundation for additional research on the elderly concerning the right-to-die and physician assisted death.

ELDERLY ACTIVISM AND PROPOSITION 161

The past two decades have witnessed an unprecedented proliferation of old-age interest groups (Day, 1990; Lammers, 1983; Liebig, 1992; Pratt, 1976). Their memberships have continued to grow, and their lobbying techniques have become more sophisticated and refined, as a result of many years of "practice" (Day, 1990; Pratt, 1976). By the early 1970s, these organizations had achieved a "fair share" of access to power, especially at the national level (Binstock, 1972). In keeping with the growing diversity of the older population, new groups sprang up to represent the socially and economically disadvantaged and various ethnic minorities, similar to interest group proliferation among the non-aged (Wolman and Teitelbaum, 1985; Liebig, 1992).

Although old-age interest groups have expanded and the share of the federal budget benefiting the elderly has continued to grow, some have questioned whether these old-age interest groups have emerged as an effective and unstoppable force in American politics and whether policy gains for elders have been the outcome of their efforts (Day, 1990; Wolman and Teitelbaum, 1985; Miller, Gurin, and Gurin, 1980). Far more agreement exists about the high levels of senior voters' awareness and voting behavior. The elderly are far more likely to vote than other age groups and participate in other ways, such as paying close attention to political news and contributing to political campaigns (Dobson, 1983; Glick, 1991).

According to some scholars, senior organizations are rarely decisive in bringing about major programs for the aged in the 1960s and 1970s; other political forces-such as the president, other elected officials, or coalition partners (e.g., labor unions)--may deserve as much or more of the credit for policy achievements (Day, 1990). Both Social Security and Medicare experienced substantial cutbacks in the 1980s, despite the strength of the "gray lobby" (Pratt, 1976) in blocking undesired changes (Liebig, 1992). Given the current policy climate in Washington, the erosion of policies benefiting the aged is likely to continue.

At the state level, old-age interest groups have been less visible, although Thomas and Hrebnar (1990) found that they are increasingly viewed as important players in state capitals. This lack of activism has been evident even when issues that are presumably germane to the interests of the elderly, such as family leave for caregivers, are being debated (Wisensale and Allison, 1988; Liebig, 1992). As Glick has noted (1991), the elderly have not sought to influence right-to-die policymaking at the state level in either the courts or the legislatures.

However, old-age interest groups have not been entirely inactive as a political force in the states. They do, in fact, testify at committee hearings when a bill is being considered, but this activity typically comes at the final stages of the legislative process, long after bills have been drafted and key sponsors and opponents have been identified (Glick, 1991). While testifying puts different groups and individuals on record as having favored or opposed a bill, it is reasonable to maintain that old-age interest groups have at best played a peripheral role in the adoption of right-to-die policies.

A comparison between the political activity of the elderly population regarding economic issues and their activity on behalf of old-age interest groups in relation to physician assisted death is revealing.[2] The American Association of Retired Persons (AARP) and the other major age-based groups have always been able to mobilize their members around national issues such as Social Security and Medicare, which together form the foundation of economic security in old age. By contrast, most state issues have been less compelling. Euthanasia and related issues have generated even less sustained advocacy than have such issues as tax relief, health care, housing, and transportation.

In the three states studied by Glick (California, Florida, and Massachusetts), elderly Californians were most active in encouraging passage of living will laws (Glick, 1991). Old-age interest groups indicated their support in 1976 by writing letters to legislative committees and Senator Keene, the bill sponsor, but they did not round up support for the legislation, and thus played an essentially passive role.

Glick relates that active senior involvement in California was evident a few years later, in 1985, when the Gray Panthers urged Senator Keene to sponsor the uniform living will law of the National Conference Commission on Uniform State Laws. The Panthers planned to coordinate support among other old-age interest groups in California, such as AARP, the Older Women's League (OWL), and others. The amendments, however, were not introduced until 1987; by then, the aging associations appear to have moved on to other issues (Glick, 1991).

In a similar fashion, AARP refrained from either endorsing or opposing Proposition 161 in 1992, primarily because of its controversial nature.[3] To keep from offending their constituency, as had occurred during the passage and subsequent repeal of the Medicare Catastrophic Care Act, for the most part AARP (and other Californian old-age interest groups) opted not to choose sides in the heated debate about whether or not an individual possesses the right to hasten his/her own death, with the aid of a physician, in the event of terminal illness. This lack of activity appears to substantiate Glick's contention that advocates for the elderly and associations of the elderly have not been prominent in drafting or supporting legislation, nor have they sought to influence the formation of judicial policy in this controversial area (Glick, 1991).

A list of endorsements compiled by the "Yes on Proposition 161" campaign revealed that only two old-age interest groups endorsed the measure: the Gray Panthers and the OWL of California. It is significant that only these two old-age nationally based organizations chose to endorse the measure, based on action by their state chapters. I conducted a telephone interview in February 1993 with Jack Nicholl, the campaign manager of "Yes on Proposition 161." He affirmed that the campaign did, in fact, make several attempts to solicit the support of the other aging interest groups. He reported that the groups were quite evasive and thus the campaign was unsuccessful in obtaining any additional endorsements. When asked why these organizations did not commit themselves visibly to this issue, he answered that Proposition 161 threatened to distract them from their main concern, namely, national health care.[4] Thus, these groups appear to have chosen to sidestep the issue of physician assisted death rather than become distracted from issues that had more immediate and compelling importance to the elderly.[5]

That the Gray Panthers and Older Women's League endorsed Proposition 161 is not surprising. Both had been somewhat active in the living will legislation in the 1970s and 1980s, and furthermore, the proposition matched their basic philosophies. As one of their primary national, state, and local goals, the Gray Panthers seek to foster the concept of aging as growth during the total life span from birth to death, to advocate fundamental social change that would eliminate injustice, discrimination, and oppression in the society, and to help create a humane society (Van Tassel and Meyer, 1992). Consequently, it is logical that the Panthers would endorse a measure that calls for a reexamination of the current definition of personal rights and the legalization of an activity, the purpose of which is to permit the option of a humane and dignified death. In a similar vein, the OWL's agenda adopted in 1990 focuses on many issues related to dignity in old age, one of which is staying in control to the end of life (Van Tassel and Meyer, 1992). In the most direct way possible, Proposition 161 sought to make this a reality, obviously a compelling reason for OWL's activism on the measure.

AARP did not commit itself to any action on Proposition 161, despite personal and legal rights being one of AARP's primary concerns, as is promoting independence, dignity, and purpose, and striving to improve the quality of life for older Americans (Van Tassel and Meyer, 1992). As noted in the organization's annual policy book, AARP state committees have broad latitude in deciding whether or not to advocate for specific issues at the state level. Even if the policy book contained a statement about euthanasia and/or related matters, any AARP state office could make its own determination about whether to support such a measure. A similar situation arose on a recent California ballot measure that sought to adopt the Canadian health care system, with government as the primary payer. AARP's state organization endorsed that proposal, although the national organization did not support a similar measure that was advanced in Washington. As an organization devoted to promoting responsible advocacy and promoting discussion of issues of importance to the elderly, AARP could conceivably have been very effective in educating the public or its membership on the pros and cons of Proposition 161, without taking sides. Instead, AARP chose not to become engaged in the issue, despite the activism of the two other old-age interest groups with which it had worked on related issues in the past.

Two statewide senior organizations--the California Association of Homes for the Aging (an organization affiliated with a national association representing residential care facilities) and the California Commission on Aging (an entity affiliated with the California Department on Aging)--formally articulated their disapproval of the physician assisted death measure. They were joined by some local organizations: the Center for Prevention of Elderly Suicide, the Mercy

Retirement and Care Center of Redding, and the San Diego Regional Home Care Council. This division among old-age interest groups, coupled with the silence of a major organization such as AARP, resulted in the elderly sending mixed and competing messages to public officials and possible allies, such as AIDS activists. As Glick (1991) notes, the right-to-die probably divides the elderly along the same religious and political lines found in the non-aged population.

A discussion of elderly activism necessitates recognition of certain political disadvantages faced by this segment of the population. Most state legislators do not perceive elderly groups as active in state politics, nor do many legislators self-identify as advocates for the elderly or specialists in aging legislation (Glick, 1991:302; Liebig, 1992). Furthermore, most senior groups do not employ professional lobbyists at the state level (Browne, 1985). Consequently, they lack the contacts that other interest groups possess as a result of hiring professional lobbyists. Lastly, the major advocacy efforts of the elderly are targeted on maintaining current policy gains and blocking any action that would affect them or their organizations adversely (Pratt, 1976; Day, 1990). Attempting major new programs, particularly those that are controversial, requires enormous energy (Glick, 1991), as does trying to get a new and innovative idea onto the political agenda. When the latter is coupled with other political disadvantages, such as lack of access, the prospects for success become disproportionately low.

The number of organizations opposing Proposition 161 was much larger than those endorsing the measure, and the opposition outspent its supporters $3 million to $285,000 ("Newsbriefs," 1992). The "No" campaign was heavily funded by Roman Catholic bishops, hospitals, and other church-affiliated groups such as the Knights of Columbus (Jacobs, 1992). Consequently, the "No" side had both the necessary funds and supporters to carry out an effective media campaign. Their stronger financial position allowed them to reach much of the public through television, rather than being forced to rely almost exclusively on print media. In this way, the less educated members of the population (who are presumably less likely to read the newspaper and/or lengthy campaign materials--Nie, Verba, and Petrocik, 1976) were more likely to hear arguments about why the measure should be defeated.

In addition, the "No" side was joined by several national professional medical organizations, including the American Cancer Society and hospice care organizations (such as National Hospice Organization), which also disseminated their own publicity on the measure. As a result, the silence of AARP and other senior organizations was not as detrimental to the "No" side as it was to the "Yes" side.[6]

SENIOR ATTITUDES ON THE RIGHT-TO-DIE

Lack of persistent effort by senior organizations concerning right-to-die issues appears to indicate that these issues are not a priority for this age group. Another way to determine possible support and interest of the elderly is to examine public opinion polls and studies of individual preferences.

Surveys of older persons' attitudes toward euthanasia and the right-to-die have produced somewhat equivocal results. Saul and Saul (1977, 1988) report that older persons, when queried about their opinions about suicide and the right-to-die, express impassioned arguments in favor of self-determination. However, Leinbach (1993), in his review of articles published in the late 1970s and the 1980s, found a consensus that older persons were more likely than younger persons to oppose euthanasia.

Polling data have helped measure individual beliefs regarding active euthanasia. A Gallup poll published in 1978 asked individuals (not stratified by age) if they thought that a person had the moral right to end his/her life when faced with an incurable disease. Forty percent of the respondents answered "yes," but a majority (53%) answered "no." In 1992, another Gallup Poll asked the respondents the same question. Fifty-eight percent replied "yes" and 36% replied "no," suggesting that the public had become more accepting of the need to address end-of-life issues. In that same poll, individuals were also asked if they thought doctors should be allowed by law to end a patient's life by some painless means if the patient and his or her family requested it; 65% answered affirmatively and 31% answered negatively.

Leinbach (1993) conducted a cohort analysis of National Opinion Research Center data. The center had asked a question about euthanasia in 1977 as part of its General Social Survey. The same question was repeated in 1978, 1982, 1983, 1985, 1986, and then yearly between 1988 and 1991. Leinbach's analysis revealed that older persons do not become less supportive of euthanasia as they age, and that the most influential predictors of attitudes are not age, but attendance at religious services, strength of religious conviction, and region of the country. Thus, it would appear from these several studies and polls that support for active euthanasia has grown, both among the general population and the elderly. The literature suggests that, in general, the level of individual senior voter awareness and support is high.

During the fall of 1992, several polls were conducted in California to measure public support for Proposition 161. The Field Poll (Field and DiCamillo, 1992), conducted on the Saturday preceding the election on Tuesday, November 3, revealed that awareness regarding the ballot proposal was indeed quite high. Statewide, 65% of those polled reported having heard about it one week prior to the election, with 29% in favor, 27% opposed, and 9% undecided. The small margin of those favoring physician assisted death over those who did not was a signal that relative levels of support had changed. The margin between supporters and opponents had been considerably wider in early September, when 19% were in favor, 10% were opposed, and 3% were undecided. These statewide results were not, however, grouped according to age. Therefore, I decided to explore senior attitudes on the issue.

THE PASADENA SENIOR CENTER SURVEY

To gauge whether senior citizens might differ from the general population on an issue of presumably greater concern to older adults, the first author administered a survey at the Pasadena Senior Center in Pasadena, California. The survey was a pre-election questionnaire to measure voter awareness about, and attitudes toward, Proposition 161. In no way representative of the senior population as a whole-since the persons surveyed and later questioned were not randomly chosen-this study afforded a "glimpse" of senior attitudes toward physician assisted death.[7]

The seniors surveyed were members of an academic group, the Senior Curriculum, that assembled every Tuesday and Thursday for 2 hours to hear lectures on politics, music, literature, and the like delivered by professors from Occidental College and the University of Southern California. To join this group, each individual was required to pay $140 for the year. A total of 200 individuals, age 50 and older, was enrolled in the program. Members of Senior Curriculum can be considered the "intellectual elite" of the Pasadena Senior Center population because of their commitment to learning, especially in later life, and their willingness to pay $140 to join the group. Their responses, therefore, would reflect a generally educated, middle or upper-class orientation.

In addressing the research question about the attitudes of the elderly with respect to Proposition 161, I hypothesized the following:

1. Gender would not be significantly related to a position on physician assisted death. Since terminal illness and death are clearly phenomena to which everyone is vulnerable, gender would presumably have little bearing upon a person's attitude toward aid-in-dying.

2. Positive attitudes toward the ballot measure (a high favorability rating) would be significantly related to party affiliation. Campbell, Converse, Miller, and Stokes found that "the strength and direction of party identification are facts of central importance in accounting for attitudes and behavior" (1960:121). This has certainly been the case with abortion, an issue that has consistently polarized Democrats and Republicans (Tatalovich, 1988). As such, the Democrats have largely supported a woman's right of choice, and Republicans, in seeking to protect the life of the unborn fetus, have been against it. Thus, I surmised that since the issues are similar-they both involve the right of choice and self-determination, albeit at opposite ends of the life cycle-self-identified Democrats would tend to support physician assisted death and Republicans would tend to oppose it.

3. A high favorability rating would be positively associated with more years of education. This hypothesis is based on the premise that those who are less educated (having acquired a high school education or less) would be less likely to read up

on the topic (see Nie, Verba, and Petrocik, 1976). Individuals who are more educated (those holding college degrees) are more likely to do their "research" into the issue by reading (newspapers, magazines, and campaign materials) and talking with their friends and family, perhaps ultimately voting in favor of the issue.

4. Religious affiliation would be closely associated with support or opposition to the measure, in keeping with Leinbach's findings (1993). I expected that those who were Catholic would be more likely to be opposed, given the opposition of the Catholic Church to similar measures (Carpenter, 1993) and specifically to Proposition 161. I also anticipated that other denominations would be more likely to embrace the concept of aid-in-dying (see Carpenter, 1993).

FINDINGS OF THE SURVEY

The first question inquired whether the respondent was previously aware that Proposition 161 was on the ballot. The survey results indicate that 129 of the 138 respondents knew that it was, seven persons did not know, and two did not reply. Of those who knew of its existence, 52% were in support of the measure, 29% were against it, 17% were undecided, and 2% did not respond. Thus, those who knew Proposition 161 was on the ballot were generally in favor of the measure. When the seven individuals who were not aware that there was a physician assisted death measure on the ballot learned of its existence, three (43%) indicated support, two (29%) indicated opposition, one was undecided, and one did not answer. Hence, one week before the election, this group of seniors was largely in favor of Proposition 161.

A series of questions asked for demographic characteristics. Respondents were asked to indicate their gender (male or female), political party identification (Democrat, Republican, other), level of educational attainment (high school, one to three years of college, college graduate, and graduate school), and religious affiliation (a "fill in the blank" question).

The survey responses by gender are presented in Table 5.1. A chi-square test of association on this data set indicates a relationship that is not significant between attitudes toward aid-in-dying and gender (as anticipated).

Table 5.1: Survey Responses by Gender

Category	N	For	Against	Undecided	No Response	Total
		(%)	(%)	(%)	(%)	(%)
Male	37	57	22	19	2	100
Female	100	51	32	15	2	100

The data shown in Table 5.2 confirm the hypothesis that a high favorability rating would be associated with party identification. The members of the Senior Curriculum group who identified themselves as Democrats were decidedly in favor of Proposition 161; Republicans, by contrast, were more likely to be opposed. A chi-square test of association indicates at a 1% level of significance that attitudes toward physician assisted death are different based on party identification.

Table 5.2: Survey Responses by Party Identification

Category	N	For	Against	Undecided	No Response	Total
		(%)	(%)	(%)	(%)	(%)
Democrat	76	59	20	21	0	100
Republican	54	41	46	11	2	100
Other	5	60	0	20	20	100

Table 5.3 shows varying results across the five educational subgroups. The chi-square test analysis indicates a significant difference in response across educational groups (5% significance level).

Table 5.3: Survey Responses by Level of Education

Category	N	For (%)	Against (%)	Undecided (%)	No Response (%)	Total (%)
High School	6	67	33	0	0	100
1-3 yrs. College	33	30	36	27	7	100
College Grad.	46	57	28	15	0	100
Grad. School	53	60	25	13	2	100

However, with respect to whether individuals actually vote, level of education may be completely insignificant for this group, for two reasons. First, retirees have decidedly more time to read, watch television, and converse with friends and family. This greater availability of time may enable them to form opinions and attitudes in a relatively thorough manner, regardless of their level of education. Second, individuals who have chosen to enroll in Senior Curriculum are considered "elite" regardless of their level of education. Given their willingness to pay $140 in support of their commitment to life-long learning, "elite" does not simply describe level of education. In fact, this sample group possesses high school graduates who are considered "elite."

When I analyzed religion and voting preference, some interesting results emerged. The survey asked the respondents to state their religious affiliation, and, as was anticipated, religion is related to whether individuals supported or opposed aid-in-dying. Twenty out of 138 respondents chose not to reply to the question. It is prudent to realize that the number of self-identified individuals in each religion subgroup is so small that the results may not be representative of the attitudes, beliefs, and values of the rest of the members of the religious subgroups outside of this study. The results are as follows (see Table 5.4):

- All seven Catholic respondents were against Proposition 161.
- A plurality of members of other Christian denominations supported the measure.
- Jewish members of the sample were overwhelmingly in favor of the measure.[8]
- Forty-four individuals fell into the "undeclared" category, indicating either that they did not follow any religion (24) or that they did not reply to this question (20). Of those persons, 27 (62%) favored Proposition 161, eight (18%) were opposed, and eight (18%) were undecided.

Table 5.4: Survey Responses by Stated Religion[9]

Category	N	For	Against	Undecided	No Response	Total
		(%)	(%)	(%)	(%)	(%)
Catholic	7	0	100	0	0	100
Other Christian	68	50	35	15	0	100
Judaism	14	71	0	21	8	100
Unclassified	5	20	20	40	20	100
None/Undeclared	44	62	18	18	2	100

Casual conversation between and with seniors on both sides of the ballot proposition further illuminated the issue. Many who were supportive believed that Proposition 161 should be passed so that they would have the right to choose in the event that they should become terminally ill. Additionally, some of their support was a by-product of the knowledge that old age is (often) a time when individuals fall prey to debilitating, life-threatening diseases. One woman, when pointedly asked why she believed in physician assisted death, referred to her arthritis and replied, "You have no idea how difficult it can be to live with acute pain day after day, knowing that it will not be getting better-only worse." Her outlook was shared by many who fear that they will be forced to stay alive, which, in their estimation, is a fate worse than death itself. Upon elaboration, she suggested that a point can be reached when life, rather than death, becomes the enemy.[10]

These follow-up conversations also revealed a general dissatisfaction with Proposition 161 and the way in which it was worded, even among those supporting the idea of aid-in-dying. Individuals were particularly concerned about the lack of safeguards. For example, the stipulation that the patient had to have made the request on two different occasions was troubling because there was no definition of the time that had to elapse between the requests.

In addition, those opposed to Proposition 161 believed that a terminally ill individual would not be able to decide the issue rationally. They felt that the individual's judgment might be tainted by depression brought on by the knowledge of impending physical and/or mental deterioration and inevitable death. These conversations also revealed that some seniors felt particularly vulnerable as older people. They expressed fear of coercion, should they be in a weakened mental state, and some believed that individuals in convalescent homes could be imperiled if physicians had the legal authority to hasten death.

These same concerns were aired in editorials and campaign advertisements during the waning days of the campaign for and against Proposition 161. The measure was defeated in the election, by roughly the same margin as the Washington initiative. An unpublished post-election analysis sponsored by the "Yes" campaign revealed that Proposition 161 received 4,562,010 "Yes" votes and 5,348,947 "No" votes. Only 43% of older voters (age 60 and older) voted "Yes," as opposed to 52% of young voters (18-29 years). This breakdown would appear to confirm earlier studies that the elderly are more likely to oppose euthanasia than younger persons (Leinbach, 1993).

In summary, old-age interest groups played at best a peripheral role in the opposition and support of Proposition 161. As discussed earlier, this was much more detrimental to the "Yes" campaign since it did not enjoy the same financial backing as did the "No" side. Furthermore, in spite of the fact that members of the senior population seemed to favor the theory behind Proposition 161, they were by and large not willing to render their total support with a "yes" vote.

The next and final chapter explores prospects for future initiatives with respect to assisted suicide.

NOTES

[1]This chapter was originally published in *Politics and Life Sciences* (September, 1996: vol.15, #2) with Phoebe S. Liebig, Ph.D.

[2]In her discussion of the ERA, Jane Mansbridge (1993) astutely asserts "organizing on behalf of the general interest usually requires volunteers, and mobilizing volunteers often requires an exaggerated, black or white vision of events to justify spending time and money on the cause" (1993, p. 6). AARP and the other major interest groups have always perceived that Social Security and Medicare are the policies around which they can generate member support (Day, 1990). These two policies form the foundation of economic security for the majority of elders.

[3]A recent presentation by Robert Binstock reports that AARP's chief lobbyist told him that the organization avoids issues such as the right-to-die because they run the risk of polarizing their members (Binstock, 1995).

[4]First Lady Hillary Rodham Clinton, in promising a comprehensive reform of health care, suggested the need to explore and answer questions such as when life should begin or end (Chen, 1993).

[5]Arguably, end-of-life decisions are central to the health care dilemma, if for no other reason than the implicit economic aspect. (See, for example, the arguments advanced by Daniel Callahan, 1987).

[6]As Glick (1991) observes, interest groups have been increasingly active in the courts and have filed briefs in right-to-die cases. Old-age interest groups, however, have not made a sustained effort to influence state public policy in the courts. Rather, those most active in submitting amicus curiae briefs have been medical organizations, including state medical societies, hospital and nursing home associations, individual hospitals, hospices, medical schools, followed by national right-to-die advocacy groups, principally the Society for the Right-to-Die and Concern for Dying.

[7]Such a study offers valuable insight into senior attitudes and opinions, especially since physician assisted death as a ballot measure, is a relatively new concept and occurrence. The first attempt at legalizing physician assisted death through the initiative process was

in California in 1988. The measure never made it onto the ballot due to lack of signatures (Humphry, 1993: 94).

[8]Carpenter (1993) notes that some rabbis have voiced strong opposition to physician aid-in-dying.

[9]The "other Christian" category includes Baptist, Christian Scientist, Congregational, Episcopal, Lutheran, Presbyterian, Unitarian, and Methodist. The "unclassified" category includes those members of the Senior Curriculum population who identified themselves as Agnostic, Infinite Way, New Thought, and Non-Sectarian. "None/Undeclared" includes individuals who did not reply (20) and those who indicated that they did not observe any religion (24).

[10]Conversation with Eleanor Perlmutter, Pasadena Senior Center member, 21 January, 1993.

VI

Prospects For Self-Deliverance

The passage of Measure 16 proves that the gestation period for physician assisted suicide had been sufficient, thus implying that this is an idea whose time had finally "come." But in the states which do not have the initiative process, can the legislatures, state and national, be expected to legalize physician aid-in-dying thereby promulgating any type of regulatory policy? Despite past legislative activity, some scholars[1] assert that the probability of government action is minimal, for the simple reason that physician assisted suicide has not precipitated the type of crisis that directly affects large numbers of people, although the increasing number of AIDS victims may very well provide the catalyst or public crisis that is necessary to elicit government attention.[2]

Additionally, policy-makers will presumably continue to avoid assuming a definitive position on the issue in an effort to refrain from polarizing their constituencies. Physician assisted suicide will always be an emotionally charged topic, one which is likely to incite passionate activity and debate, much like abortion. Politicians will refrain from squarely confronting legalization of assisted suicide in order to avoid being labeled for or against. Consequently, complete and total patient autonomy, or the lack thereof, will probably remain unaddressed (but not necessarily unrecognized) within state and national legislatures.

The courts, being passive institutions, may be the ultimate vehicle for legalizing physician aid-in-dying, especially since the courts will have the last say as to whether Measure 16 and other future initiatives are enacted.

MAKING STRIDES

It is probable that as the topic of assisted suicide continues to gain people's attention, one can expect to witness increasing activity, since individuals will inevitably develop stronger opinions and attitudes. In addition, the increasing prevalence of terminal diseases, such as AIDS and cancer, which continue to rob patients of their mental and physical dignity in the later stages of the illness, will also be responsible for the heightened activity of family, friends and patient advocacy groups, such as Compassion in Dying. Perhaps the existence and activities of this group will inspire the formation of similar organizations. The fact that such an organization is in existence lends credence to the fact that the movement is gaining momentum and that there is a demand for aid-in-dying. Even more convincing is that although the Roman Catholic Archdiocese of Seattle and other right-to-life organizations denounce the actions of Compassion in Dying, the backlash has not been as vehement as one would expect.[3]

What can also be expected is greater support from physicians for two reasons. First, they are the ones who must treat these terminally ill patients, whose pain the physician *may or may not* be able to control, but whose quality of life the physician absolutely *cannot* restore. Secondly, medical schools incorporate ethical issues such as physician aid-in-dying into their curricula, thereby compelling medical students to reflect upon whether or not acting in a humane manner includes helping patients to die. The fact that this highly relevant but controversial topic is introduced in the classroom setting renders it inevitable that a certain segment of "younger" physicians will embrace assisted death in theory and in practice.

One can also depend on the activities of Dr. Kevorkian to keep the issue center stage. In this way, he is clearly furthering, rather than impeding the movement. Had it not been for Dr. Kevorkian and his strong convictions which prompted him to aid in forty-one deaths as of September 1996, physician assisted death might still be on the periphery. His actions have, however, been considered drastic and perhaps what is most troubling about Dr. Kevorkian's activities is that he does not limit his aid to those who are terminally ill. This makes some members of the public uncomfortable because his decision-making process for who will receive his help seems entirely too subjective. Again, both Propositions 119 and 161 and Measure 16 advanced the right to hasten death only if it is imminent within six months.

In spite of this, the reality is that every movement needs a pioneer like Dr. Kevorkian to focus public attention and expose the pros and cons of the issue. Especially since Dr. Kevorkian has been able to avoid being convicted, he will continue to play a central role in forcing the public to continue to think about physician assisted suicide and in promoting patient autonomy. For example, in August, 1996, Kevorkian and his attorney, Geoffrey Fieger, filed suit in Federal District Court in Detroit to have a 1994 state Supreme Court ruling that physician assisted suicide could be a common law crime found in violation of the U.S. Constitution (Lessenberry, 8/17/96: A6).

INTERNATIONAL ACTIVITIES

On July 1, 1996, more than one year after the regional legislature passed a bill sanctioning its use, voluntary euthanasia became legal in the Northern Territory of Australia. Physicians, however, refused to use the law until the a ruling had been rendered by the Northern Territory Supreme Court. The law, which allows physicians to administer lethal doses of drugs to the terminally ill, was challenged by the Australian Medical Association and aboriginal religious groups. In a two to one ruling, the Northern Territory Supreme Court upheld the law. Dr. Chris Wake, Chairman of the Coalition Against Euthanasia and member of the region's medical association indicated that the ruling would be appealed to the High Court of Australia.

The Northern Territory Rights of the Terminally Ill Act has twenty-two steps which must be followed when a patient requests aid-in-dying. Specifically, the guidelines require that a psychiatric opinion, as well as explicit consideration of palliative care as an option (*Arizona Republic*, 1996). Additionally, several physicians must be involved and the patient's request must endure over at least nine days. Similar to Measure 16, voluntary euthanasia is only permitted for competent, terminally ill adults.

While the physician assisted suicide debate continues to rage in the U.S. and other countries, the Netherlands have permitted inducing death for the terminally ill for more than a decade, provided that guidelines, originally written in 1984, are met. Technically, euthanasia is not legal in the Netherlands, but many Dutch physicians have helped patients to die by administering a drug overdose through injection or intravenous drip knowing that they will not be prosecuted.

In August 1995, new guidelines regarding the practice of voluntary active euthanasia were drawn up by doctors, lawyers and ethicists were sent out to the members of the Royal Dutch Medical Association (Simons, 1995). One of the most striking changes was the recommendation that the terminally ill patient should administer the fatal drug to themselves, rather than the physician actually hastening the patient's death. Furthermore, no doctor is required to perform euthanasia. Equally important, the new refinements include the requirement that physicians ask for a second opinion from another experienced physician, a rule that physicians say has largely been ignored (Simons, 1995). The new guidelines were the result of feedback from doctors who said that they feel too much pressure from patients and sometimes colleagues to engage in euthanasia when they personally oppose it or when they are not sure the circumstances are appropriate (Simons, 1995).

Finally, in Canada in 1993, Sue Rodriguez, a woman suffering from advanced amyotrophic lateral sclerosis (ALS), filed suit asserting that British Columbia's law prohibiting assisted suicide violated her liberty and security under the Canadian Charter of Rights and Freedoms, which is similar to the Bill of Rights. On September 30, 1993 by a vote of 5 to 4, the Supreme Court of Canada ruled against Sue Rodriguez stating that she does not have the right to physician aid-in-dying because that would compromise "our fundamental conception of the sanctity of life" (Kondro, 1993). Too disabled to take her own life, the Court acknowledged that while the prohibition deprives Rodriguez "of autonomy over her person and causes her physical pain and psychological distress....fundamental justice required that a fair balance be struck between the interests of the state and those of the individual" (Kondro, 1993).

While the decision was disappointing for Sue Rodriguez, the controversy surrounding the case was useful for the purpose of posing the question regarding legalization of physician assisted suicide to Canadian citizens. In this way, the gestation process continues in Canada. Perhaps rejection of Sue Rodriguez's request to have assistance in dying will encourage legislative or interest group activity for the purpose of legalization.

FUTURE ACTIVITY

Based on California's experience with Proposition 161 and the findings of the senior center survey, what can be expected in the future of old-age interest groups and elderly individuals on the topic of physician assisted death? This case study has shown that the major old-age interest groups are hesitant to either endorse or oppose measures sanctioning active euthanasia, largely because the topic is controversial. Organizational survival requires that these groups not offend their membership (Day, 1990). Their stance is not likely to change, because so many moral, religious, and social factors surround the aid-in-dying issue. However, one of the important tasks of old-age interest groups is to educate their members and the general public about issues that have particular relevance for the elderly. The right-to-die issue will become even more salient in the next century, given the accelerated aging of the U.S. population and growing concerns about the costs of caring for many more frail older persons, especially in the last years of life (Callahan, 1987). If major interest groups such as AARP were to provide a forum for the discussion of this and similar issues, both the general public and the elderly would benefit. Older voters especially look to their interest groups for voting cues or more information.

This research also suggests that while elderly individuals, such as the Pasadena seniors, have rather strong feelings about active euthanasia and favor physician assisted death, they are wary of the specifics of any public policy dealing with these issues. In this regard, they do not differ from the general population, if anecdotal accounts in the popular media can be trusted. Confirming Leinbach's research (1993), conversations with Pasadena Senior Center members demonstrated that seniors seemed to favor the concept of assisted-death, but when faced with a specific initiative, they were less favorably inclined.

Given the multidimensional and compelling nature of this issue, further study that incorporates other variables, such as age, is warranted. Furthermore, since this is a topic that continues to surface at the state level, additional survey research of the Oregon experience would be worthwhile.

Since the prospect of dying is a difficult reality, physician assisted suicide will probably always be a sensitive subject for the elderly. Consequently, it is not reasonable to expect that the elderly will emerge as a strong political force advocating physician assisted death. While they may favor legalizing physician aid-in-dying, activities that represent a push for legalization may prove too close for comfort.

It is necessary, however, for the elderly to be much more active in seeking memberships of interest groups, to devote more of their energies to activities such as lobbying, if they wish to obtain more political victories (Glick, 1991: 302) and to help tailor future policies to their liking. The latter is particularly important if their interests and concerns are to be incorporated into policies. Since the senior population comprises such a significant portion of the politically active population, group membership would be valuable to the extent that it would inspire the type of goal oriented activity that is necessary to promote passage of any measure.

Furthermore, while the Pasadena Senior Center survey did not yield "representative" results, it did serve the purpose of identifying what barriers exist in "selling" assisted suicide to the public, particularly the elderly population. In this way, it is useful for future strategizing techniques. It is important to realize that self-deliverance may always be a sensitive issue for the elderly since the denial that one is going to die someday continues to be a difficult reality. Consequently, it is probably not reasonable or prudent to expect that the elderly will emerge as a strong political force advocating assisted suicide. While they may be in favor of legalizing physician aid-in-dying, activities which represent a push for legalization may prove too close for comfort.

In addition, an integral part of the gestation and timing of physician assisted suicide for senior members of the population involves encouraging them to avail of current options (e.g., advance directives, the durable power of attorney, and the DNR order). This can only be done by educating seniors. Presumably, this was the intent of the Patient Self-Determination Act. But as discussed in Chapter Two, the Act is not achieving its desired results. This in itself is note-worthy, and should be a signal to policy-makers that the Act needs to be revised so that individuals, particularly members of the senior population, make important end-of-life decisions under appropriate circumstances.

Furthermore, if physician assisted suicide is to become legalized in other states, ballot initiatives need to appeal to the more "conservative" religious denominations, such as the Catholic church, in some way so that assisted suicide is not interpreted as killing, *per se*. Additionally, it is this sector of the population which should be the target of increased and intensive campaigning efforts. In fact, the success of Measure 16 may be due in large part to the fact that Oregon has the second-lowest percentage of church-goers in the country (*The Economist*, 11/26/94).

The problem of definitions should also be underscored. In addition to defining what it means to "kill" someone, concepts such as what it means to be "dead" and what constitutes a "good" or "bad" quality of life need to be clarified so that there is general agreement as to their meanings. As long as lucidity is lacking in terms of definitions, one cannot expect that reflective and definitive attitudes toward the topic will be cultivated.

With these thoughts in mind, one has to wonder if the state by state adoption of advance directives can be considered a predictor of the path physician assisted suicide will take. As discussed briefly in Chapter Four, the work of Henry Glick serves as a useful indicator. Glick first posits that the initial adoption of a policy in one state eventually spreads throughout other states, and that the policy may not spread uniformly (Glick, 1991). Rather, policy-making may exhibit initial innovation, varied diffusion and reinvention over time (Glick & Hayes, 1991: 836). In other words, in adopting a particular law, states may choose to alter or "reinvent" the content of a certain policy issue. While this is significant, perhaps what is even more important is the fact that according to Glick, policy-making sometimes mimics the ripple effect. For example, *Quinlan* was a seminal case since, up until that time, there was no legislative or appellate judicial policy concerning the rights of individuals to end life-prolonging treatment (Glick, 1990). Following this case, however, additional litigation flowed into the state courts, and state legislatures began to enact living will laws (Glick, 1990: 75). When confronted with a similar issue, courts in other states frequently looked to the *Quinlan* decision, making it the second most frequently cited case (Glick, 1990).[4] Glick asserts that what takes place is judicial innovation and policy re-invention in that judges specifically refer to precedents which frequently influence a policy outcome. For example, the Massachusetts Supreme Judicial Court followed New Jersey's application of the right to privacy in the 1977 case, *Superintendent of Belchertown State School, et al. v. Joseph Saikewicz*, but in doing so, it created a distinctive policy of its own (Glick, 1990: 85).

In a similar way, regarding assisted suicide, one might hypothesize that once a certain standard is used to legalize aid-in-dying, the process of re-invention may take place and what might be witnessed is similar ballot initiatives in different states sanctioning its legalization. Glick's analysis seems to tacitly imply that policy innovation and policy re-invention need not only take place *via* the courts (1990). Instead, other policy-making vehicles, such as direct democracy, may witness similar patterns since the courts have made few strides in this area.

As discussed in Chapter Four, Proposition 161 was clearly a refined version of the earlier Washington State Proposition 119, supporting Glick's re-invention theory. As discussed, it was not an exact replica of the Washington state initiative. Instead, it was decidedly more specific and a few of the provisions had been altered in an effort to discourage potential abuses. This type of modeling phenomenon is quite likely for the future, especially considering the cases of Washington, California and Oregon.

It is clear that the physician assisted suicide cause as a whole would benefit from additional research. In hindsight, the literature lacks in-depth discussion about how issues which evolve into social movements, such as physician assisted suicide, fare within the context of the initiative process. Specifically, is it mandatory that successful ballot measures be preceded by a social movement or does the emotion inspired by social movements cloud issues so much that defeat is often the outcome? As such, it would be worthwhile to explore the particular elements of the physician assisted suicide (social) movement and which components contributed to the defeat of the first two ballot measures and the success of the last one.

The right-to-die literature was disturbingly devoid of substantial scholarly support for the rights of dying AIDS patients. The literature is sufficient for the purposes of educating the public as to how AIDS qualifies as a terminal illness and the effects of the debilitating virus. What is lacking is someone within the academic realm to champion the cause. It is simply not enough for AIDS activists alone to try and educate the public about the agonies associated with the last stages of the illness. Rather, the message also needs to be delivered within the intellectual/academic arena in an attempt to hasten passage of a law sanctioning physician assisted death.

What also merits some further examination is whether or not the initiative process is the best venue for resolving politically delicate issues. The physician assisted suicide example points to the possibility that this may indeed be the case given that the formal policy-making institutions have basically backed away from the issue, although the Supreme Court's activity in *Roe v. Wade* certainly suggests the contrary.

Finally, in addition to further research, future efforts at legalizing aid-in-dying will be useful for the obvious purpose of gauging public interest as well as for determining other problematic areas. It is only by trial and error that the inherent difficulties will be resolved. If the history of this issue is any indication, no matter how precisely other initiatives are written, many attempts will be required in each state before physician assisted suicide is legalized and enacted.

References

Admiraal, P.V. (1986). "Active Voluntary Euthanasia." In A.B. Downing & Barbara Smoker (eds.), *Voluntary Euthanasia: Experts Debate the Right to Die*. London: Humanities Press International, Inc.

Admiraal, P.V. (1989). "Justifiable Active Euthanasia in the Netherlands." In Robert M. Baird and Stuart E. Rosenbaum (eds.), *Euthanasia: The Moral Issues*. New York: Prometheus Books.

Alexander, H.E. and N. Bhojwani (1991). "Term Limits and Election Reform" Prepared for Term Limits Conference, 31 May-1 June, University of California, Irvine

Arant, D. (1992). "No Dignity in "Death with Dignity." *Glendale News Press* (30 September): A17.

Armstrong, A. (1987). "Can a "Life Advocate" Impair the Constitutional Right to Reject Life-Prolonging Medical Treatment?" *Cumberland Law Review* 17: 553-568.

"Australians Launch Challenge of Voluntary Euthanasia Law." (1996). *Arizona Republic* (14 June): A28.

Balzar, J. (1994). "Northwest Group Issues Quiet Call for Legalized Assisted Suicide." *Los Angeles Times* (31 March): A5.

Barnes, J.A. (1990). "Losing the Initiative." *National Journal*. (1 September): 2046-53.

Barrington, M.R. (1990). "Euthanasia: An English Perspective." In Arthur S. Berger & Joyce Berger (Eds.), *To Die or Not to Die? Cross-Disciplinary, Cultural, and Legal Perspectives on the Right to Choose Death*. Westport, Connecticut: Praeger.

Bartholow, J. (1992). "When Death is Certain, Choice Should Prevail." *Register Pajaronian*. (8 July): 18.

Bartling v. Superior Court (1984) 163 Cal. App. 3d 186, 209 Cal. Rptr. 220 (Ct. Appl.).

Bartling v. Glendale Adventist Medical Center (1986) 184 Cal. App. 3d 97, 228 Cal. Rptr.847 (Ct. App.).

Battin, M. (1992). "Assisted Suicide: Can We Learn from Germany?" *Hastings Center Report.* 22 (March-April): 44-51.

Baumgartner, F.R. and B.D. Jones (1993). *Agendas and Instability in American Politics.* Chicago: University of Chicago Press.

Beisser, A.R. (1990). *A Graceful Passage.* New York: Doubleday.

Bell, Charles and C. Price (1988). "Are Ballot Measures the Magic Ride to Success?" *California Journal* 19 (September) 380-384.

Belluck, P. (1996). "Man Expected to Go to Prison for Helping Wife Kill Herself." *New York Times* (16 March): B23 & 26.

Bender, L. (1992). "A Feminist Analysis of Physician-Assisted Dying and Voluntary Active Euthanasia." *Tennessee Law Review.* 59 (3): 519-546.

Berger, A.S. (1990). "Last Rights: The View from a U.S. Courthouse." In Arthur S. Berger & Joyce Berger (eds.), *To Die or Not to Die? Cross Disciplinary, Cultural, and Legal Perspectives on the Right to Choose Death.* Westport, Connecticut: Praeger.

Berger, Arthur S. (1993). *Dying and Death in Law and Medicine.* Westport, Connecticut: Praeger.

Berk, K.S. (1992). "Mercy Killing and the Slayer Rule: Should the Legislatures Change Something?" *Tulane Law Review* (December) 67: 485-507.

Beyette, B. (1992). "The Reluctant Survivor" *Los Angeles Times* 13 September: E1 &7.

"Bill to Ban Assisted Suicides Okd by Michigan Legislature." (1992). *Los Angeles Times* (4 December): A2.

Binstock, R.H. (1972). "Interest Group Liberalism and the Politics of Aging." *The Gerontologist* (Part 1): 265-80.

Binstock, R.H. (1983). "The Aged As Scapegoat." *The Gerontologist* 23: 136-143.

Binstock, R.H. (1995). "Health Care Policy and Older Americans." Paper presented at the annual meeting of the American Political Science Association, Chicago, IL.

Bopp, J., Jr. (1987). "Is Assisted Suicide Constitutionally Protected?" *Issues in Law and Medicine* 3 (2): 113-140.

Bosso, C.J. (1994). "The Practice and Study of Policy Formation." In Stuart S. Nagel (ed.), *Encyclopedia of Policy Studies.* New York: Marcel Dekker.

Bostick, W.L. and C.R. Koons (1992). "Embrace a Chance to Ease Life's Final Suffering." *Los Angeles Times* (16 September): B7.

Bouvia v. Superior Court (Glenchur) (1986) 225 Ca. Rptr. 297 (Cal. App. 2 Dist).

Bouvia v. Los Angeles County (1987) 241Cal. Rptr. 239 (Cal. App. 2 Dist.).

Boyle, P. (1991). "Vote Shows that Euthanasia will go On." *Los Angeles Times*, (9 November): F17.

Brahams, D. (1984). "The Right to be Allowed to Die: Self Induced Starvation and the Right to Die Without Undue Misery." *Medico-Legal Journal* 52 (Spring): 113-116.

Brock, D.W. (1992). "Voluntary Active Euthanasia." *Hastings Center Report* 22 (2) (March-April): 10-22.

Browne, W. P. (1985). "Variations on the Behavior and Style of State Lobbyists and Interest Groups." *Journal of Politics* 47: 450-468.

Browne, W.P. (1990). "Organized Interests and Their Issue Niches: A Search for Pluralism in a Policy Domain." *Journal of Politics* 52 (2): 477-509.

Buckley, W.F. (1994). "Deciding Who Lives or Dies, With a Twist." *Los Angeles Times* (8 May): M15.

Burns, H. (1996). "The Legal Landscape of Physician Aid in Dying." Hemlock Society Promotional Material. (15 April).

Callahan, D. (1987). *Setting Limits: Medical Goals in an Aging Society*. New York: Simon and Schuster.

Callahan, D. (1992). "When Self-Determination Runs Amok." *Hastings Center Report* 22 (2) (March-April): 52-55.

Campbell, A., Converse, P.E., Miller, W.E. and D.E. Stokes. (1960). *The American Voter*. New York: John Wiley and Sons.

Campbell, C.S., J. Hare, and P. Matthews (1995). "Conflicts of Conscience: Hospice and Assisted Suicide." *Hastings Center Report* 25 (3) (May-June): 36-43.

Cantor, N.L. (1973). "A Patient's Decision to Decline Life-Saving Medical Treatment: Bodily Integrity Versus The Preservation of Life." *Rutgers Law Review* 26: 229-264.

Capron, A.M. (1992). "Substituting Our Judgment." *Hastings Center Report* 22 (2) (March-April): 58-59.

Carpenter, B.D. (1993). "A Review and New Look at Ethical Suicide in Advanced Age." *The Gerontologist* 33: 359-65.

"Catholic Groups Effectively Kill Bill to Legalize Assisted Suicide." (1995) *Providence Journal-Bulletin* (8 May): C1.

Cassel, C.K. and D,E. Meier (1990). "Morals and Moralism in the Debate Over Euthanasia and Assisted Suicide." *New England Journal of Medicine* 323 (3): 750-753.

Cheever, J. (1986). "Waiting For Death With Dignity." *New Jersey Law Journal* 117 (2): 1, 7, & 56.

Chen, E. (1993). "Reality Deepens Hillary Clinton's Cause." *Los Angeles Times* (7 March): A1.

Cobb, R.W. and C.D. Elder (1983). *Participation in American Politics.* Baltimore: The Johns Hopkins University Press.

Coleman, G. (1989). "Assisted Suicide: An Ethical Perspective." In Robert M. Baird and Stuart E. Rosenbaum (eds.), *Euthanasia: The Moral Issues.*

Compassion In Dying v. State of Washington (1995) 49 F. 3d 586.

Conner, D. (1994). "Assisted Suicide Ban in Washington Struck Down." *Los Angeles Times* (4 May): A7.

Cotton, P. (1991). "Providers to Advise of "Medical Miranda."" *Journal of the American Medical Association* 265 (3) (16 January): 306.

Coyle, M. (1990). "Is the Court Avoiding the Big Question?" *The National Law Journal* (9 July): 1 & 24.

Cox, G.W. and S. Kernell (1991). *The Politics of Divided Government.* San Francisco: Westview Press.

Cronin, T.E. (1989). *Direct Democracy.* Cambridge: Harvard University Press.

Cruzan v. Harmon (1988) 760 S.W. 2d 408.

Cruzan v. Director, Missouri Department of Health (1990) 497 U.S. 261, 110 S. Ct. 2841.

Daar, J.F. (1995). "Direct Democracy and Bioethical Choices: Voting Life and Death at the Ballot Box." *University of Michigan Journal of Law Reform* 799 (Summer): 799-899.

Danis, Marion, L.I. Southerland, J.M.Garrett, J.L. Smith, F. Hielema, C.G. Pickard, D.M. Enger, and D.L. Patrick (1991). "A Prospective Study of Advance Directives for Life-Sustaining Care." *The New England Journal of Medicine* 324 (13) (28 March): 882-888.

Day, C. (1990). *What Older Americans Think: Interest Groups and Aging Policy.* Princeton, N.J.: Princeton University Press.

David, R. and J.Brierley (1978). *Major Legal Systems in the World Today.* (2nd ed.). New York: The Free Press.

Davidson, K.W., C. Hackler, D.R. Caradine, and R.S. McCord (1989). "Physicians' Attitudes on Advance Directives." *Journal of the American Medical Association* 262 (17) (3 November): 2415-2419.

deWachter M.A.M. (1992). "Euthanasia in the Netherlands." *Hastings Center Report* 22 (2): 23-33.

Dickey, N.W. (1993). "Euthanasia: A Concept Whose Time Has Come?" *Issues in Law and Medicine* 8: 521- 532.

Dobson, D. (1983). "The Elderly as a Political Force." In W.P. Browne and L.K. Olson (eds.), *Aging and Public Policy*. Westport, CT: Greenwood.

Dolan, M. (1993). "Ill May Refuse Efforts to Save Life, Court Says." *Los Angeles Times* (27 July): A1 & A15.

"Dr. Kevorkian Arrested After Witnessing Cancer Patient's Suicide." (1993). *Los Angeles Times* (17 May): A16.

Dunleavy, P. (1988). "Group Identities and Individual Influence: Reconstructing the Theory of Interest Groups." *British Journal of Political Science* 18: 21-49.

Dworkin, R. (1993). "The Price of Life: How High the Cost Before it Becomes Too High?" *Los Angeles Times* (29 August): M1 &M6.

Ecker, M. (1993). "Playing God With a Baby's Life." *Los Angeles Times* (31 October): M5.

Emanuel, LL., M.J. Barry, J.D. Stoeckle, L. Ettleson, and E.J. Ezkiel (1991). "Advance Directives For Medical Care - A Case for Greater Use." *The New England Journal of Medicine* 324 (13) (28 March): 889-895.

Enright, D.J. (1983). *The Oxford Book of Death*. Oxford: Oxford University Press.

Enriquez, S. and H. Blume (1992). "Victim of Freeway Shooting Talks of Despair, Suicide." *Los Angeles Times* (23 December): A1 & A20.

Estes, C.L. (1979). *The Aging Enterprise*. San Francisco: Jossey-Bass.

Eule, J.N. (1990). "Judicial Review of Direct Democracy." *Yale Law Review* 99: 1503-1587.

Farah, J. (1992). "A Broad Hint to Get Out of the Way." *Los Angeles Times* (14 September): B5.

Field, M. and M. DiCamillo (1992). *The Field Poll.* San Francisco: The Field Institute.

Fletcher, J. (1989). "Sanctity of Life versus Quality of Life." In Robert M. Baird and Stuart E. Rosenbaum (eds.), *Euthanasia: The Moral Issues.* pps. 85-95.

Friess, S. (1996). "Uneasy Alliance." *The Advocate* 5 March: 46-48.

Gallup, G. (1978). *The Gallup Poll.* DE: Scholarly Resources, Inc.

Gallup, G. (1984). *The Gallup Poll.* DE: Scholarly Resources, Inc.

Gallup, G. (1992). *The Gallup Poll.* Wilmington, DE: Scholarly Resources, Inc.

Gamble, E., P.J. McDonald, and P.R. Lichstein (1991). "Knowledge, Attitudes, and Behavior of Elderly Persons Regarding Living Wills." *Arch Intern Med* 151: 277-280.

Gaylin, W., L.R. Kass, E.D. Pellegrino, and M. Siegler. (1989). "Doctors Must Not Kill." In Robert M. Baird and Stuart E. Rosenbaum (eds.), *Euthanasia: The Moral Issues.* New York: Prometheus Books.

Gibbs, N. (1992). "Mercy's Friend or Foe?" *Time* (28 December): 36-37.

Gilbert v. State (1986) 487 So. 2d 1185 (Fla. Dist Ct. App.).

Gill, C.J. (1992). "Deciding Whose Life Has Value." *Los Angeles Times* (21 October): B7.

Giliam, J. (1993). "Term Limits Put Assembly 27 On Bipartisan Path." *Los Angeles* (15 March): A1 & A17.

Girsh, F.J. (1992). "Physician Aid in Dying: A Proposed Law for California." *Criminal Justice Journal* 14 (2) (Fall): 333-334.

Gleicher, E. (1994). "Legalized Physician-Assisted Suicide." *Michigan Bar Journal* 73 (2): 184 & 186.

Glick, H. (1991). "The Right to Die: State Policymaking and the Elderly." *Journal of Aging Studies* 5 (3): 283-307.

Glick, H. (1990). "Judicial Innovation and Policy Reinvention: State Supreme Courts and the Right to Die." *The Western Political Quarterly* 71-91.

Glick, H. and S.P. Hays (1991). "Innovation and Reinvention in State Policymaking: Theory and the Evolution of Living Will Laws." *Journal of Politics* 53 (3) (August): 835-849.

Glick, H. (1992). *The Right to Die: Policy Innovation and Its Consequences.* New York: Columbia University Press.

Gray, V. (1973). "Innovation in the States: A Diffusion Study." *American Political Science Review* 67: 1174-1185.

Gray, W.A., R.J. Capone, and A.S. Most, (1991). "Unsuccessful Emergency Medical Resuscitation: Are Continued Efforts in the Emergency Department Justified?" *New England Journal of Medicine* 325 (20): 1393-1397.

Griswold v. Connecticut (1965) 381 U.S. 497.

Gross, J. (1993). "At AIDS Epicenter, Seeking Swift, Sure Death." *New York Times* (20 June): 10.

Hackler, C., and F.C. Hiller (1990). "Family Consent to Orders Not to Resuscitate." *Journal of the American Medical Association* 264 (10): 1281-1283.

Hager, P. (1991). "Term Limits Upheld By Supreme Court." *Los Angeles Times* (11 October): A1 & A34.

Hager, P. and D.G. Savage (1991). "New Tests for Oldest Liberties." *Los Angeles Times* (13 December): A1.

Hanna, W.J. (1981). "Advocacy and the Elderly." In Richard H. Davis (ed.), *Aging: Prospects and Issues* (3rd ed.), Los Angeles, CA: University of Southern California Press.

Harris, S. (1993). "A Hard Lesson on Death and Dying." *Los Angeles Times* (7 October): B2.

Hill, P.T. and D. Shirley(1992). *A Good Death*. New York: Addison-Wesley Publishing Company, Inc.

Hirsch, D.E. (1990). "Euthanasia: Is it Murder or Mercy Killing? A Comparison of the Criminal Laws in the United States, the Netherlands and Switzerland." *Loyola of Los Angeles International and Comparative Law Journal* 12: 821-843.

Hoefler, J. and B. Kamoie (1992). "The Right to Die: State Courts Lead where Legislatures Fear to Tread." *Law & Policy* 14:(4): 337-380.

Hoefler, J. and B. Kamoie (1994). *Deathright*. Boulder: Westview Press.

Hoehne, J.L. (1993). "Physician Responsibility and the Right to "Death Care": The Call For Physician-Assisted Suicide." *Drake Law Review* 42: 225-253.

Humphry, D. (1981). *Let Me Die Before I Wake*. 5th Edition. Eugene: The Hemlock Society.

Humphry, D. (1991). *Final Exit*. New York: Dell Publishing.

Humphry, D. (1992). *Dying With Dignity*. New York: Carol Publishing Group.

Humphry, D. (1993). *Lawful Exit*. Junction City, OR.: The Norris Lane Press.

Humphry, D. and A. Wickett (1991). *The Right to Die*. Eugene: The Hemlock Society.

"It's Over, Debbie." (1988). *Journal of the American Medical Association* 259 (January): 272.

Iverson, K.V. (1989). "Case Studies: Pre-hospital DNR Orders." *Hastings Center Report* 19: 17-19.

Jacob, H. (1988). *The Silent Revolution*. Chicago: University of Chicago Press.

Jacobs, P. (1992). "Emotions Run High Over Doctor-Aided Death Issue." *Los Angeles Times* (24 October): A1 & A24.

Jacobs, P. (1992). "Outcome of Death Measure May Rest on 11th-Hour Ads." *Los Angeles Times* (28 October): A1 & A16.

Jacobs, P. (1992). "Prop. 161: A Matter of Life or Death at the Polling Place." *Los Angeles Times* (10 October): A20 & A26.

Jacobs, P. (1992). "Quietly, Doctors Already Help Terminal Patients Die." *Los Angeles Times* (29 September): A1 & A20.

Jacobs, P. (1992). "Suicide measure Losing Cash Battle." *Los Angeles Times* (18 October): A3 & A21.

Jacobs, P. and D.M. Weintraub (1991). "Lawmakers Say Ruling Will Shift Power in Sacramento." *Los Angeles Times* (11 October): A30 & A31.

Jones, T. (1993). "Setting a Date for Death." *Los Angeles Times* (14 March): A1, A8 & A10.

Jones, T. (1992). "Netherlands Law Sets Guidelines for Euthanasia." *Los Angeles Times* (10 February): A1 & A8.

Jost, K. (1992). "Term Limits." *CQ Researcher* 2: (10 January): 3-23.

Kamisar, Y. (1958). "Some Non-Religious Views Against Proposed "Mercy-Killing" Legislation." *Minnesota Law Review* 42 (6) (May): 1043.

Kamisar, Y. (1989). "Right to Die or License to Kill?" *New Jersey Law Review* 124 (21): 7 & 16-19.

Kamisar, Y. (1994). "The "Right To Die": A Catchy But Confusing Slogan." *Michigan Bar Journal* 73 (2): 184-185.

Keown, J. (1992). "On Regulating Death." *Hastings Center Report* 22 (2) (March-April): 39-43.

Kevorkian, J. (1991). *Prescription: Medicide: The Goodness of Planned Death.* New York: Prometheus Books.

"Kevorkian Assists in Suicides of Two Elderly Cancer Victims." (1993). *Los Angeles Times* (5 February): A14.

"Kevorkian Jurors Focus on Suicide Consent Form." (1994). *Los Angeles* (30 April): A30.

"Kevorkian Assists Woman From New Jersey in Dying." (1996). *New York Times* (12 June): A20.

Key, V.O., Jr. (1955). "A Theory of Critical Elections." *Journal of Politics* 17: 3-18.

Kingdon, J.W. (1984). *Agendas, Alternatives, and Public Policies.* Glenview, Illinois: Scott, Foresman and Company.

Knox, Richard. 1991. "Washington State Voters Reject Proposal to Legalize Euthanasia." *Boston Globe.* (Boston, Mass.), 7 November: C3.

Kondro, W. (1993). "Court Rules Against Physician-Assisted Suicide." *The Lancet* 342: 9 October, 918-919.

Koop, C.E. (1989). "The Right to Die: The Moral Dilemmas." In Robert M. Baird and Stuart E. Rosenbaum (eds.), *Euthanasia: The Moral Issues.* New York: Prometheus Books.

Krauthammer, C. (1993). "Let Kevorkian Get His Wish - On Kevorkian." *Los Angeles Times* (5 December): M5.

Lace, T. (1989). "The Physician Can Play a Positive Role in Euthanasia." *Journal of the American Medical Association* 262 (21): 1 December, 3075.

Lammers, W.W. (1983). *Public Policy and Aging.* Washington, D.C.: Congressional Quarterly, Inc.

Law, S. (1996). "Physician Assisted Death: An Essay on Constitutional Rights and Remedies." *Maryland Law Review* 55: 292-342.

Lee v. State of Oregon (1995) 891 F. Supp. 1421.

Leinbach, R.L. (1993). "Euthanasia Attitudes of Older Persons." *Research on Aging* 15: 433-48.

Lessenberry, J. (1993). "Jack Kevorkian: Defending Assisted Suicide Right Up To The End." *Los Angeles Times* (12 December): M3.

Lessenberry, J. (1996). "After Victory, A New Trial For a Weary Kevorkian." *New York Times* (11 March): A13.

Lessenberry, J. (1996). "Jury Acquits Kevorkian in Common-Law Case." *New York Times* (15 May): A14.

Lessenberry, J. (1996). "Kevorkian Goes From Making Waves to Making Barely a Ripple." *New York Times* (17 August): A6.

Lewin, T. (1996). "Suits Accuse Medical Community of Ignoring "Right to Die" Orders." *New York Times* (2 June): A1 & A28.

Liebig, P.S. (1992). "Federalism and Aging Policy in the 1980s: Implications for Changing Interest Group Roles in the 1990s." *Journal of Aging Social Policy* 4(1/2): 17-33.

Llewellyn, D.L. Jr. (1992). "Licensed to Kill: The "Death with Dignity" Initiative." *Criminal Justice Journal* 14 (2): 309-332.

Logue, B.J. (1993). *Last Rights: Death Control and the Elderly in America*. New York: Lexington Books.

Magleby, D. (1984). *Direct Legislation*. Baltimore: Johns Hopkins University Press.

Magleby, D. (1986). "Legislatures and the Initiative: The Politics of Direct Democracy." *Journal of State Government* 59 (1): 31-39.

Mansbridge, J. (1986). *Why We Lost the ERA*. Chicago: University of Chicago Press.

Marek, T. (1992). "November Ballot Measure Legalizes Doctors' Aid in Dying For Terminally Ill." *San Carlos-Belmont Enquirer Bulletin* (22 July): A10.

Matthews, M.A. (1987). "Suicidal Competence and the Patient's Right to Refuse Lifesaving Treatment." *California Law Review* 75 (2) (March): 707-758.

Meier, Diane E. (1991). "The Physician's Experience: Elderly Patients." *The Mount Sinai Journal of Medicine* 58: 385-387.

Miller, A.H., P. Gurin, and G. Gurin. (1980). "Age Consciousness and Political Mobilization of Older Americans." *Gerontologist* 20 (6): 691-700.

Montalvo, B. (1991). "The Patient Chose to Die: Why?" *The Gerontologist* 31 (5): 700-703.

Moore, W.J. (1988). "Election Day Lawmaking." *National Journal* (17 September): 2296-2301.

"Murder Charges Against Kevorkian Are Dismissed." (1992). *New York Times* (New York, N.Y.) (22 July): A6.

Neugarten, B.L. (1982). "Older People: A Profile." In Bernice L. Neugarten (ed.), *Age or Need? Public Policies for Older People*. Beverly Hills, CA: SAGE Publications, Inc.

"Newsbriefs." (1992). *Aging Today* 13 (6) (Nov/Dec): 2.

Nie, N.S., S. Verba, and J. Petrocik. (1976). *The Changing American Voter*. Cambridge: Harvard University Press.

Nuland, S.B. (1994). *How We Die: Reflections on Life's Final Chapter*. New York: Alfred Knopf.

"Oregon's Goodnight." (1994). *The Economist* 333 (891) (26 November): 28.

"Other Doctors to Help Woman in Pain, Kevorkian Lawyer Says." (1994). *Los Angeles Times* (30 March): A33.

Painton, F. (1987). "Tolerance Finally Finds Its Limits." *Time* 130 (9): 31 August: 8 & 29.

Pasternack, J. (1993). "Michigan Brings Charges Against Suicide Doctor." *Los Angeles Times* (18 August): A1 & A12.

Pasternack, J. (1993). "Showdown in Kevorkian Case Seems Near." *Los Angeles Times*, (26 October): A8.

Pasternack, J. (1994). "Kevorkian's Assisted-Suicide Trial Opens." *Los Angeles Times* (20 April): A1 & A21.

Pasternack, J. (1994). "Kevorkian Compares His Actions to Those of Gandhi." *Los Angeles Times* (28 April): A18.

Pasternack, J. (1994). "Kevorkian Is Acquitted for Role in Suicide." *Los Angeles Times* (3 May): A1 & A17.

Pasternack, J. and T. Shryer (1993). "Kevorkian, Facing Trial, Present at Suicide." *Los Angeles Times* (11 September): A2.

Pasternack, J. and T. Shryer (1993). "Rational Suicide Ruling Clouds Kevorkian Case." *Los Angeles Times* (14 December): A26.

People v. Roberts (1920) 211 Mich. 187, 178 N.W.

People v. Kevorkian (1994) 447 Mich. 436, 527 N.W.2d 714.

Peters, P.G., Jr. (1989). "The State's Interest in the Preservation of Life: From *Quinlan* to *Cruzan*." *Ohio State Law Journal* 50: 890-977.

Peterson, G.W. (1985). "Right to Die." *Pepperdine Law Review* 13: 111-154.

Peterson, P.E. (1990-91). "The Rise and Fall of Special Interest Politics." *Political Science Quarterly* 105 (4): 539-556.

Pickering, J. (1989). "Preserve Life, But Not "At All Costs."" *New Jersey Law Review* 124 (21) 7 & 17.

Platte, M. and L. Hall (1993). "Kevorkian Aids Two from Southland in Their Suicides." *Los Angeles Times* (19 February): A3 & A26.

Post, S.G. (1993). "How Shall the Aged Die?" *The Gerontologist* 33: 427-29.

Pratt, H.J. 1976. *The Gray Lobby*. Chicago: University of Chicago Press.

Pratt, H.J. (1983)." National Interest Groups Among the Elderly: Consolidation and Constraint." In W.P. Browne and L.K. Olsen (eds.), *Aging and Public Policy*. Greenwood Press.

Pletcher, R.A. (1992). "Assisted Suicide for the Terminally Ill: The Inadequacy of Current Legal Models to Rationally Analyze Voluntary Active Euthanasia." *Criminal Justice Journal* 13: 303-317.

Podgers, J. (1992). "Matters of Life and Death: Debate Grows Over Euthanasia." *American Bar Association Journal* (May): 60-63.

President's Commission for the Study of Ethical Problems in Medicine and Biomedical and Behavioral Research. *Deciding to Forego Life-Sustaining Treatment*. (1983). Washington, D.C.: U.S. Government Printing Office.

Price, C.M. (1975). "The Initiative: A Comparative State Analysis and Reassessment of a Western Phenomenon." *Western Political Quarterly* 28: 243-262.

Price, C. and R.Waste (1991). "Initiatives: Too Much of a Good Thing?" *California Journal* 22: 117-120.

"Prosecutor of Kevorkian Loses Re-election Bid." (1996). *New York Times* (8 August): A23.

Quill, T.E. (1993). *Death and Dignity: Making Choices and Taking Charge*. New York: W.W. Norton & Company.

Quill v. Vacco (1996) 80 F.3d 716.

In re Quinlan (1976). 97 N.J. S. Ct. 319.

Rachels, J. (1989). "Active and Passive Euthanasia." In Robert M. Baird and Stuart E. Rosenbaum. (Eds.), *Euthanasia: The Moral Issues*. New York: Prometheus Books.

Remlink Committee Report (1991) *Lancet* 338: (14 September): 669-74.

Renteln, A.D. (1993). "A Justification Of The Cultural Defense As Partial Excuse." *Southern California Review of Law and Women's Studies* 2 (2): 437-526.

Rice, C.E. (1994). "Committing "Rational" Suicide." *The New American* 21 February: 35.

Risely, R. and M. White (1992). *The California Death With Dignity Act*. California Civil Code, Title 10.5, Sections 2525-2525.24.

Rochefort, D. and R.W. Cobb (1994). "Problem Definition: An Emerging Perspective." In David A. Rochefort and Roger W. Cobb (eds.), *The Politics of Problem Definition: Shaping the Policy Agenda*. Lawrence: University Press of Kansas.

Rodriguez v. British Columbia (Attorney General) (1993) 3 R.C.S. 519.

Roe v. Wade (1973) 140 U.S. 113.

Rollin, B. (1985). *Last Wish*. New York: Warner Books.

Roy, F.H. and C. Russel (1992). *The Encyclopedia of Aging and the Elderly*. New York: Facts on File.

Ross, M. (1992). " '92 Voters Better Informed, Survey Finds." *Los Angeles Times* (15 November): A25.

Rusk, J.G. (1976). "Political Participation in America: A Review Essay." *American Political Science Review* 70: 583-591.

Salisbury, R.H., J.P. Heinz, E.O. Laumann, and R.L. Nelson. (1987). "Who Works With Whom? Group Alliances and Opposition." *American Political Science Review* 81 (4): 1217-1234.

Satz v. Perlmutter (1978) 47 Fla. Supp. 190 (Brownard County Circuit Court).

Satz v. Perlmutter (1978) 362 So. 2d 160 (Fla. Dist Ct. App.).

Satz v. Perlmutter (1980) 379 So. 2d 359 (Fla.).

Saul, S. and S. Saul. (1988). "Old People Talk about Suicide: A Discussion about Suicide in a Long-Term Care Facility for Frail and Elderly People." *Omega* 19: 237-51.

Sayid, M. (1983). "Euthanasia: A Comparison of the Criminal Laws of Germany, Switzerland and the United States." *Boston College International and Comparative Law Review* 6 (2): 533-562.

Schaffer, C.D. (1986). "Criminal Liability for Assisting Suicide." *Columbia Law Review* 86 (2) (March): 348-376.

Schanker, D.R. (1993). "Of Suicide Machines, Euthanasia Legislation, and the Health Care Crisis." *Indiana Law Journal* 68 (3): 977-1010.

Schloendorff v. Society of New York Hospital (1914) 80 F.3d 716.

Schmidt, D. (1989). *Citizen Lawmakers*. Philadelphia: Temple University Press.

Serrell, N. (1994). "Poll Shows Physician Support For Assisted Suicide." *Valley News* (18 September): A1 & A4.

Shapiro, M. (1981). *Courts.* Chicago: University of Chicago Press.

Shapiro, M.H. and R.G. Speece, Jr. (1981). *Bioethics and Law.* St. Paul: West Publishing Co.

Sherlock, R. (1982). "For Everything There is a Season: The Right to Die in the United States." *Brigham Young University Law Review* (3): 545-616.

Shewmon, A.D. (1987). "Active Voluntary Euthanasia: A Needless Pandora's Box." In Robert M. Baird and Stuart E. Rosenbaum (eds.), *Euthanasia: The Moral Issues.* New York: Prometheus Books.

Siegel, M. and J. Nicholl (1992). Unpublished Post Election Analysis.

Simons, M.. (1995). "Dutch Doctors to Tighten Rules on Mercy Killings." *New York Times* (11 September): A3.

Smith, C.K. (1993). "What about Assisted Suicide?" *Issues in Law and Medicine* 8 (4) (Spring): 503-519.

Smith, G.P. (1989). "All's Well That Ends Well: Toward a Policy of Assisted Rational Suicide or Merely Enlightened Self-Determination?" *University of California, Davis Law Journal* 22: 275-419.

State v. Bouse, (1953) 199 Ore.S. Ct. 676; 264 P.2d 800.

Tallian, L. (1977). *Direct Democracy.* Los Angeles: People's Lobby Press.

Tatalovich, R. (1988). "Abortion." In R. Tatalovich and B.W. Daynes (eds.), *Social Regulatory Policy.* Boulder, CO: Westview Press

ten Have, Henk A.M.J. and Jos V.M. Welie, (1992). "Euthanasia: Normal Medical Practice?" *Hastings Center Report* 22 (2) (March-April): 34-38.

Thomas, C.S. and R.J. Hrebnar (1990). "Interest Groups in the States." In C. Gray, H. Jacob, and R.B. Albritton (eds.), *Politics in the American States,* 5ᵗʰ edition. New York: HarperCollins.

"Too Much, Too Little for the Dying." (1993). *AARP Bulletin* 34 (2) (February): 5.

Tomlinson, K.A. (1988). "The Right of the Elderly to Self-Determnation and New York's Legislative Imperative." *Pace Law Review* 8 (63): 63-113.

Ubel, P.A. (1993). "Assisted Suicide and the Case of Dr. Quill and Diane." *Issues in Law and Medicine* 8 (4) (Spring): 487-502.

Union Pacific Railroad v. Botsford (1891) 141 U.S. 250, 251.

United States House of Representatives, Select Committee on Aging. (1985) *Dying with Dignity: Difficult Times, Difficult Choices.* (October) Washington: U.S. Government Printing Office.

United States v. Salerno (1987) 481 U.S. 745.

Uzych, L. (1993). "Knocking On Death's Door." *Pennsylvania Law Journal* 26 (37): 2 & 18.

Van Tassel, D.D. and J.E.W. Meyer (1992). *Aging Interest Policy Groups.* Westport, CT: Greenwood Press.

Verba, S. and N.H. Nie, (1972). *Participation in America.* New York: Harper & Row.

Walker, J. (1969). "The Diffusion of Innovations Among the American States." *American Political Science Review* 63: 880-899.

Walker, J.L. (1983). "The Origins and Maintenance of Interest Groups in America." *American Political Science Review* 77: 390-405.

Walsh, E. (1993). "Kevorkian Helps Physician Kill Self." *Valley News* (23 November): B1.

Walsh, E. (1994). "Michigan Commission Favors Legal Physician-Assisted Suicide." *Los Angeles Times*, (26 April): A14.

Warrick, P. 1993. "Right to Die Law Prompts Mix-Ups." *Los Angeles Times* (12 January): E1 & E8.

Warrick, P. (1992). "Suicide's Partner." *Los Angeles Times* (6 December): E1, E8 & E9.

Warrick, P. (1993). "Choosing Not to Die Alone." *Los Angeles Times* (30 March): E1 & E2.

Walters, J.W. (1992). "When Dying is Human, Humane." *Los Angeles Times* (18 October): M5.

Warrick, P. (1993). "Right to Die Law Prompts Mix-Ups." *Los Angeles Times* (12 January): E1 & E8.

Warrick, P. (1992). "Suicide's Partner." *Los Angeles Times* (6 December): E1, E8 & E9.

Warrick, P. (1993). "Choosing Not to Die Alone." *Los Angeles* (30 March): E1 & E2.

"What is the "Good Death?" (1991) *The Economist* (20July): 21-24.

White, M.L. and J.C. Fletcher (1991). "The Patient Self-Determination Act-On Balance, More Help Than Hindrance." *Journal of the American Medical Association.* 266: 410-412.

Williams, G. (1957). *The Sanctity of Life and the Criminal Law.* New York: Knopf.

Wilson, J.A. (1991). "In Washington, They Hate Californians More Than Politics." *Los Angeles Times* (10 November): M6.

Wise, C.R. (1991). *The Dynamics of Legislation.* San Francisco: Jossey-Bass Publishers.

Wisensale, S.K. and M.D. Allison (1988). "An Analysis of 1987 State Family Leave Legislation: Implications for Caregivers of the Elderly." *The Gerontologist* 28: 779-85.

Wolhandler, S.J. (1984). "Voluntary Active Euthanasia for the Terminally Ill And The Constitutional Right to Privacy." *Cornell Law Review* 69 (2) (January): 363-383.

Wolman, H. and F. Teitelbaum, (1985). "Interest Groups and the Reagan Presidency." In L. Salamon and M. Lund (eds.), *The Reagan Presidency and the Governing of America.* Washington, D.C: Urban Institute.

Worsnop, R.L. (1992). "Assisted Suicide." *Hastings Center Report* 22 (7) (February): 145-167.

"Yes on Proposition 161." (1992). Unpublished Post Election Analysis.

Young, E.W. D. (1989). "Assisting Suicide: An Ethical Perspective." In Robert M. Baird and Stuart E. Rosenbaum, (eds.), *Euthanasia: The Moral Issues.*

Zisk, B. (1987). *Money, Media, and the Grassroots.* Beverly Hills: Sage Publications, Inc.

Zisser, P. (1988). "Euthanasia and the Right to Die: Holland and the United States Face The Dilemma." *New York Law School Journal of International and Comparative Law* 9: 361-377.

INTERVIEWS

Nicholl, J. (1993). "Yes on Proposition 161" Campaign Manager. Interview with Author: 27 February.

Perlmutter, Eleanor. (1993). Pasadena Senior Center Member. Interview with Author: 21 January.

Thomas, Griffith. (1996). Attorney and Friend of Elizabeth Bouvia. Interview with Author: 14 August.

Index